rowing the
ATLANTIC

Lessons

Learned

on the

Open Ocean

Roz

Savage

Simon & Schuster Paperbacks

New York   London   Toronto   Sydney

Simon & Schuster Paperbacks
A Division of Simon & Schuster, Inc.
1230 Avenue of the Americas
New York, NY 10020

First Simon & Schuster trade paperback edition October 2010

SIMON & SCHUSTER PAPERBACKS and colophon are
registered trademarks of Simon & Schuster, Inc.

For information about special discounts for bulk purchases,
please contact Simon & Schuster Special Sales at
1-866-506-1949 or business@simonandschuster.com.

The Simon & Schuster Speakers Bureau can bring authors
to your live event. For more information or to book an event,
contact the Simon & Schuster Speakers Bureau at
1-866-248-3049 or visit our website at www.simonspeakers.com.

Designed by Nancy Singer

Manufactured in the United States of America

10 9 8 7 6 5 4 3 2 1

The Library of Congress has cataloged the hardcover edition as follows:

Savage, Roz, date.
      Rowing the Atlantic: lessons learned on the open ocean / Roz Savage.
         p.   cm.
      1. Savage, Roz, date. 2. Rowers—Great Britain—Biography. 3. Women
   rowers—Great Britain—Biography. 4. Atlantic Rowing Race (2005)
   I. Title.

GV790.92.S26A3   2009
797.123092—dc22   [B] 2009002326
ISBN 978-1-4165-8328-8
ISBN 978-1-4391-5372-7 (pbk)
ISBN 978-1-4165-8360-8 (ebook)

This book is dedicated

to anybody who has a dream

CONTENTS

one The Unlikely Adventurer   1

two Passing the Point of No Return   9

three Beginnings   23

four What Was I Thinking?   33

five Baring My Soul—and More   43

six One Stroke at a Time   59

seven One Oar Down   79

eight Clouds of Anxiety   97

nine Life Is Easier in the Storms   109

ten Happy Birthday to Me   127

eleven All I Want for Christmas   133

twelve Rogue Wave Rumble   141

thirteen Going Garbo   155

fourteen Atlantic Hardcore   161

fifteen Between the Devil and the Deep Blue Sea   169

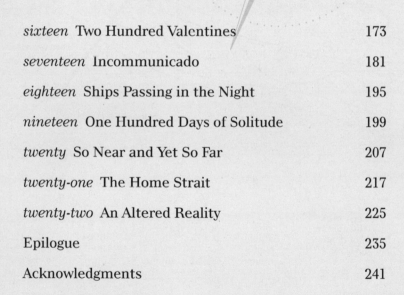

sixteen Two Hundred Valentines 173

seventeen Incommunicado 181

eighteen Ships Passing in the Night 195

nineteen One Hundred Days of Solitude 199

twenty So Near and Yet So Far 207

twenty-one The Home Strait 217

twenty-two An Altered Reality 225

Epilogue 235

Acknowledgments 241

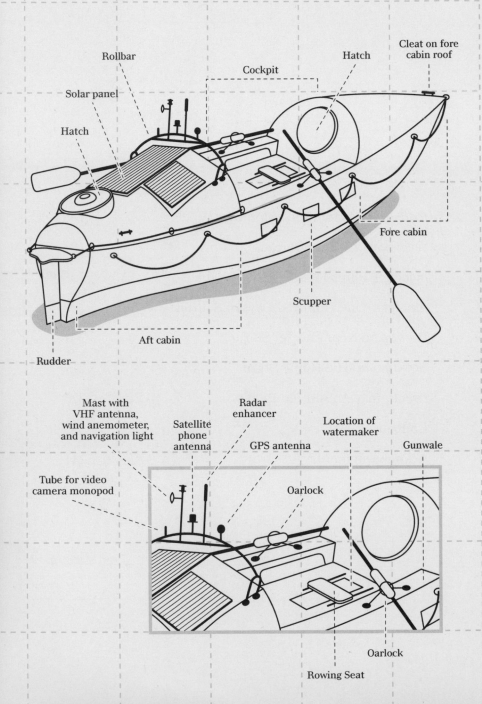

Rollbar

Solar panel

Hatch

Cockpit

Hatch

Cleat on fore cabin roof

Fore cabin

Scupper

Aft cabin

Rudder

Mast with VHF antenna, wind anemometer, and navigation light

Satellite phone antenna

Radar enhancer

GPS antenna

Location of watermaker

Gunwale

Tube for video camera monopod

Oarlock

Oarlock

Rowing Seat

rowing the

ATLANTIC

one

THE UNLIKELY ADVENTURER

a gale is blowing, and the small marina of La Gomera is haunted by a restless energy. The wind whistles through the yachts' rigging with a whispered scream, and the halyards clank mournfully against the masts as the boats jostle and strain at their mooring ropes as if yearning to be at sea. It takes only a small effort of the imagination to picture the ghosts of ancient mariners flitting among the tethered vessels, urging them to throw off their lines and leave the safety of the harbor to dare the open ocean.

Lined up alongside a pontoon on the landward side of the marina is a cluster of strange, mastless boats. They huddle together for mutual support like the oddball branch of a family at a wedding, shunned by their elegant, affluent cousins. In the darkness it is just possible to make out their unconventional livery of gaudy colors and loud patterns—one painted with huge multicolored polka dots, another with the black-and-white splotches of a Friesian cow, others in green, or orange, or hot pink.

These boats do not appear to yearn for the open ocean as their masted relatives do. In fact, they appear barely seaworthy. They have no sails and no engine; their only means of propulsion is by oar, powered by human muscle. And one of them, the *Sedna Solo,* belongs to me.

It is the evening of Tuesday, November 29, 2005, the night before the start of the Atlantic Rowing Race, and I am sitting cross-legged on the floor of *Sedna*'s tiny cabin, feeling her bump against the pontoon on one side and another rowboat on the other. My ears strain against the howl of the wind for any sounds of scraping or chafing against the structure of my precious craft, and I pop my head out of the hatch every few minutes, into the darkness of the blustery night, to make sure *Sedna*'s fragile hull is not suffering damage.

The next day, twenty-six crews will set out to row three thousand miles across the Atlantic Ocean, from the Canary Islands, a few miles from the west coast of Africa, to Antigua in the Caribbean. They will make no landfall on the way, nor will they be resupplied. Every crew has to be entirely self-sufficient for the duration of the crossing.

The race organizers describe this as "The World's Toughest Rowing Race," and in a modern world where superlatives are losing their impact, in this case the superlative is no exaggeration. Many previous attempts have foundered due to storms, breakages, injury, psychological problems, and catastrophic capsizes. Some ocean rowers have even paid the ultimate price. The pages of statistics on the website of the Ocean Rowing Society include a short but poignant list of names, titled "Lost at Sea."

What reward awaits the winner? Nothing but a cheap medal and the knowledge that they have done something out of the ordinary.

Unsurprisingly, ocean rowing is not a majority sport. Since records began, fewer than three hundred people have rowed across the Atlantic, with most of them crossing in crews of two, although there have also been a few crews of four and, out there at the lunatic fringe of this most lunatic of sports, a tiny minority of people who chose to go it alone, adding the psychological challenge of solitude to the already formidable physical, technical, financial, and logistical challenges of rowing an ocean.

For reasons that make perfect sense to me, but to few of my friends and family, I have chosen to try to join this obscure tribe of individualists. I will be the only solo female entrant in this year's Atlantic Rowing Race, and the first solo woman ever to compete in the event since it was first held in 1997. Five other women have rowed solo across the Atlantic, but those have all been independent expeditions—no woman has before pitted herself against other crews.

I ponder on this sobering fact as I sit in my cabin, rocking gently with the movement of the boat as the strong wind ruffles the usually calm waters of the sheltered marina. From the moment, fourteen months ago, when I first decided that I was going to do this, I have thought of little else. And yet, have I really thought about it at all? I have thought about what equipment I need, what food to bring, what course to navigate—but I still really have no idea what I am letting myself in for. There is nothing in my previous life that has prepared me for the reality of spending between fifty and one hundred and twenty days alone on the ocean. I know very little about what lies ahead. Until the race begins, my immediate future is simply unknowable.

....

In case you have formed the impression that I am some kind of athlete, adventurer, or adrenaline junkie, I should make clear at the outset my near total lack of qualifications for this undertaking.

First, I am not naturally sporty. If there is such a thing as a runner's high, then it has so far eluded me. I get a quicker, easier high from a chocolate chip cookie than I do from a twenty-mile run and I only took up rowing in college so I could eat more without putting on weight. If you were to pass me in the street, you would not take me for an athlete. Most rowers are tall and powerfully built. I am neither. I am just under five-foot-four, with an unfortunate tendency to tubbiness.

I am also not naturally adventurous. I had spent most of my adult life working in an office—eleven years as a project manager in the information technology industry—before deciding at age thirty-six to reinvent myself as an adventurer.

Many explorers give the impression that they emerged from the womb with ice axe, kayak paddle, or trekking pole already in hand, and it is merely a matter of time before they live out their preordained destiny. During the many years that I was an armchair adventurer, enjoying books about polar explorers, mountaineers, and round-the-world sailors, it seemed to me that these people were a breed apart, some kind of superspecies specially bred to cope with danger and extreme conditions without so much as a flicker of their steely-eyed gaze. With few exceptions they were mostly men, so I seemed to lack all the credentials to be an adventurer—physical stature, bottomless courage, and a frost-encrusted beard. Female role models were in short supply, and for most of my life it did not occur to me that I could ever join this intrepid elite of daredevils.

And yet here I am, about to row across a huge expanse of ocean, alone and unsupported. For however long it takes me to row three thousand miles, I will have nobody to rely on but myself. Rowing the Atlantic will be a huge leap of faith—or folly.

The cabin of my specially designed rowboat is cozily lit by the yellow glow from the chart light, and the red LED of my camcorder is on. I am supposed to be taping my video journal, but I don't know what to say. I search inside myself, trying to find words to describe how I feel about the challenge that lies ahead. I am not excited. I am not fired up on adrenaline. If I really think about it, I can summon up a faint flutter of nerves, but my overriding sensation is one of wonderment that I have made it this far, and a reluctance to think too deeply about what is to come lest I scare myself out of it. I start to talk.

"This is where it stops being about spreadsheets and designs and rowing on a rowing machine. This is where it starts being about rowing on the Atlantic Ocean," I say to the little red light. "I'm not sure if I really understand the full implications of that yet. If I did, I suspect I'd be doing the sensible thing and running a mile in the opposite direction. Why am I doing this? What is it all for?"

I pause for a moment, uncertain of the answer to my rhetorical question.

"So a bunch of lunatics decide to go row an ocean," I continue. "Big deal. Why should anybody else care? But they do. When I've been working on my boat here in La Gomera, this small island in the Canaries, just off the coast of Morocco, I often turn around to find a small crowd of people watching. They seem to be fascinated, asking questions and taking photos. This challenge somehow seems to strike a chord with them even though they would never want to do it themselves. Maybe we need people who are willing to go out and do something a bit crazy, just to make everyone else believe that they could do something extraordinary, too, if they wanted to. Maybe it reminds us that anything is possible, and our only limits are the ones we place on ourselves."

I hit the off button. I'm not sure who I am trying to convince—myself or a hypothetical audience. Is there any sense at all in what I am doing, or is it all just a spectacular waste of time, effort, and a modest-sized divorce settlement?

Deep down I know that this project is perfect for me. I may be struggling to put it into words, but I feel that this is exactly the right thing to do, and the right time to be doing it, and that rowing the Atlantic is the logical, almost inescapable conclusion to the series of defining moments in my life that have brought me to this place.

....

I lean back and try to find a comfortable sitting position. I fail. At its widest my cabin is about the width of a queen-size bed, but tapered down at the boat's stern to a mere one foot across. If I sit at the highest part, in front of the circular hatch that leads out to the rowing cockpit, I can just about sit upright. On either side of me the ceiling curves down toward the floor of the cabin.

My living quarters are cramped, but they are well organized. I survey with satisfaction my tiny home—the plastic box containing my dehydrated rations for the first week, the wooden control panel with its array of instruments—the small screen of a Global Positioning System chart plotter, a marine radio, a stereo amplifier. Below the control panel cabinet is a small yellow waterproof case that houses a palmtop computer and satellite phone. Once I am out of sight of land, this phone will be my only means of communication. As well as delivering the usual voice and text services, I can also use it as a modem for the computer so that I can post dispatches to my website, sending photos and text via the network of satellites that orbit the earth.

I fiddle restlessly, rearranging a few of the small items stowed in the fabric wall pockets—pens, recharger cables, notebook, sunglasses—and straighten the sleeping bag on the thin mattress of my bunk. I look at the jumbled array of notes and photographs Velcroed to the cabin wall, laminated in plastic to protect them from seawater.

The notes mostly describe emergency procedures—Mayday calls, how to deploy a life raft, reminders on how to use a VHF radio. I have never been to sea alone before, and I want to be sure that even if I am sleep-deprived and panic-stricken I won't forget what to do.

Among the photos is a passport-sized picture of the blond, good-looking guy that I have been dating. He is the apprentice from the boatyard in England that fitted out my boat. Cute, smart, fun. And nineteen years old, just half my age. He joined me here in La Gomera for a week and provided a welcome distraction, as well as practical assistance in putting the finishing touches to my boat. But as the start of the race approached I became increasingly preoccupied, and to our mutual relief, he left a few days ago to go home. In retrospect it seems a little undignified for me to be involved with somebody so young. Am I turning into a female version of the male midlife crisis cliché? A pretty and significantly younger partner, a radical change of life direction, an expensive new toy. The only difference is that my toy is a not a shiny new Porsche but a gleaming, sleek, silver ocean rowing boat.

Next to the boyfriend is a photo of my mother, Rita, and a photo of me and my younger sister, Tanya, in the back garden at Mum's small house in the north of England. The picture was taken as a present for my father, a Methodist minister, on his seventy-fifth birthday just over a year ago. We framed it and placed it on the nightstand next to his hospital bed in Leeds General Infirmary, where he lay dying. He had suffered a stroke three weeks previously, and would die three weeks after his birthday. Since his death I have become much closer to my mother. I look at her smiling serenely back at me from her photo on the cabin wall, and silently thank her for being there for me and, despite her recent widowhood, for finding the strength to give her wholehearted support to my endeavor.

I wonder when I will see my friends and family again, and whether I will miss them during my self-imposed solitary confinement. I think about the other things I will miss—mountains and landscapes, the sound of the wind in the trees, crisp sheets on a bed that stays still, hot showers, freedom and spontaneity, fresh fruit and vegetables, iced drinks, coffee shops and cookies. I sigh. I haven't even left shore yet, and already I am yearning to return to terra firma.

But, I remind myself, this is my perfect project, the logical culmination of the changes that I have been making in my life over the previous few years. I have come a long way already—from a dissatisfied office worker, miserable and unfulfilled in the routine of her workday life, to someone who is starting to believe that her dreams can come true. The ocean seems to offer many things that I want right now: peace and quiet, a chance to think and reflect on the tumultuous changes of the last few years, and an opportunity to find out who I am and what I can do. I have high hopes for the voyage. And in place of the things I will miss, I expect to find new pleasures—seeing stars thousands of miles from the nearest light pollution, cloud watching, time alone with my thoughts, a fresh perspective on the world and on myself, the joy of routine and discipline, satisfaction in rising to new challenges, self-sufficiency, self-confidence and self-awareness—high hopes indeed, and only time will tell if they will be fulfilled.

This story is my attempt to describe those hopes and what became of them, to explain what drove a thirty-eight-year-old office worker to abandon home, husband, and a comfortably secure existence to seek adventure on the high seas; I'd also like to try to pass on a few of the lessons that I learned during my journey—about life, about myself, and about what it takes to make a dream come true.

two

PASSING THE POINT OF NO RETURN

*t*he flat gray light of early dawn was spreading slowly across my cabin from the aft hatch above my head when my eyes flickered open on Wednesday, November 30. Race day had arrived. I had slept fitfully the night before, my mind churning over details that I had already pondered a thousand times, until I wanted to knock myself unconscious just to get off the repetitive treadmill of my thoughts.

By the time I had eaten my breakfast of fruit and yogurt—making the most of fresh food while I could—the sun had risen and the marina was waking up to the arrival of rowers and their entourages of families and friends. As the sun rose higher in the sky, the energy level in the marina rose, too. The air seemed charged with the cumulative tension of all sixty competitors, until it became too intense for my comfort. I decided to go somewhere less oppressive with expectancy and took myself into town on a spurious errand to get some coffee.

I found a café in the town square and sat in the shade of the trees outside to sip my cup of sweet coffee, killing time and calming myself. I watched some children running and playing in the sunshine, calling to each other and playing hide-and-seek around the sturdy tree trunks. The normality of the scene seemed surreal and strange. My sense of anticipation, mixed with a fair dose of trepidation, was so strong that it seemed that the children should be able to see it and feel it like an aura radiating from me, filling the entire town square. To my agitated mind it seemed inappropriate that they were behaving as if this was a day just like any other, when for me it was such a momentous watershed. I felt like an alien, separated from the ordinary world, letting go of the ties that bound me to it as I prepared for the biggest adventure of my life.

I finished my cup of coffee and walked slowly back to the marina. When I arrived at my boat, the representative from the watermaker company was waiting for me. This made me nervous. The watermaker was without a doubt the most important piece of equipment I had on board. During the months ahead this would be my main source of fresh water for drinking, washing, and reconstituting freeze-dried meals. If the watermaker failed, I had seventy-five liters (twenty gallons) of water stowed in plastic bottles below decks. This reserve supply would buy me time while I tried to fix the problem, or to call for a resupply if I failed. The bottled water doubled as ballast; by stowing it as far down as possible in the hull it kept the vessel's center of gravity low and would help the boat to self-right if it capsized. If the watermaker failed and I ran out of ballast water, I also had a backup manual watermaker, but this was truly a last resort as it would take several hours a day to manually pump enough water to keep me alive. Four hours of pumping as well as twelve hours of rowing would be a punishing schedule, so I was desperately eager that the watermaker should perform reliably. I'd invested £3,500 (about $7,000 U.S.) for the most expensive but most efficient and dependable watermaker on the market, which was now installed in a hatch beneath my rowing position. The machine consisted of a pipe connected to an intake hole in the hull of my boat. This pipe would draw in seawater, which would then pass through a series of increasingly fine filters and a reverse osmosis membrane to extract sediment, pollutants, and salt, until the water was purer than most tap water.

A few days earlier the watermaker representative had come to inspect my installation and had found that I was missing an important control valve that would allow me to flush the system with fresh water to keep it clean. We had resolved the issue, I thought, but now, just hours before the race was to start, here he was again, and he wanted to install a new filter. I was reluctant to let him touch it. This last-minute tweaking was rattling my confidence. But he was supposedly the expert, so I let him go ahead.

"Don't start it up yet," he advised. "The water here in the marina is too mucky and will just gunk up your new filter. Wait until you get a mile or so out into the open water and then start it up. Don't worry about it—it'll be fine."

There was now just one hour before the race was due to start, and time was starting to accelerate as the long-awaited moment approached. I retreated to my cabin to change into my race day outfit. I had been urged by my ocean rowing mentors to bulk up in advance because most ocean rowers lose a lot of weight during the crossing. I was about fifteen pounds over my usual weight and it felt strange, as if I'd woken up one morning in somebody else's body. I had some smart new sports outfits of Lycra shorts and crop top, donated by Fourth Element, a sponsor, but I was self-conscious about the extra weight I had gained in the run-up to the race and there was no way I was going to appear in a sports bikini until I was well out of sight of land. So I put on an old blue tank top and a pair of calf-length running pants. I tied my hair back into a ponytail and topped it with a baseball cap to keep the sun out of my eyes.

I turned on the amplifier and scrolled through the playlists on my iPod to find the compilation I'd prepared for today, titled "Launch." "Shine on You Crazy Diamond" by Pink Floyd issued from the speakers positioned inside the cabin and outside in the cockpit. The words seemed uncomfortably poignant.

> *Come on you target for faraway laughter,*
> *Come on you stranger, you legend, you martyr, and shine!*

Were faraway people laughing at me? I wondered. I suddenly saw my grand adventure in a different light, and felt faintly sick at the thought of how it might appear to others. I am just an ordinary woman. I'm not an adventurer. Anything could happen to me out there. I must look ridiculous. I had thought this was an inspired dream, but is it instead the height of arrogance and stupidity?

I thought to myself, come on, you crazy diamond—this is not a productive line of thought only a few minutes before the start. I pushed the negative voice of Self-Doubt away and reemerged from my cabin into the bright sunlight.

Some of the more gregarious rowers were ambling along the pontoon, wishing luck to the other competitors and hugging them good-bye. Others were keeping to themselves, focusing on last-minute preparations or just sitting quietly and thinking about what lay ahead. I didn't mind thanking the passing well-wishers but I didn't go out of my way to be sociable. I felt subdued and introverted and couldn't think what words would be appropriate to the occasion. "Good luck—have a good one" seemed too low-key. Not knowing what to say, I mostly kept my mouth shut.

The weather was warm and sunny, with a helpful breeze coming from the northeast. The crews were due to be sent off one at a time from the pontoons, to row out of the marina and into the harbor. The race start was an imaginary line drawn between the end of the harbor wall and a buoy. The boats would assemble behind the line and synchronize their approaches, aiming to cross it as the starter gun fired at eleven o'clock.

I was scheduled to be last to leave the pontoons—probably because I was the only solo woman competing in the race, and hence expected to be the slowest rower and the race organizers, Woodvale, didn't want me to obstruct the twenty-five other crews. Those crews comprised a solo man, two crews of four men, two crews of four women, and twenty pairs of various configurations of the sexes.

I didn't like being the last to cast off. I knew that over the days, weeks, and months ahead, a few minutes lost at the start line would make no practical difference, but psychologically it didn't feel good to be playing catch-up from the very beginning. I was aware that others simply assumed that I would be last to finish, so I could have lowered my sights and conformed to their expectations. But I hoped to do better.

One by one, the other crews cast off their mooring lines and paddled out of the marina. At last it was my turn. The marina was quiet and deserted. All the well-wishers were now standing on the harbor wall, facing out toward the start line and waving the crews off. Since my support team—namely my mother—had had to leave a few days earlier, my only companion was a blond forty-something Swedish journalist called Astrid who had interviewed me the day before and had offered to untie my boat lines for me.

I set up my camcorder on its mount on the roof of my cabin so I could tape the start of the race. I pressed the record button and took my seat. I pulled on my white kangaroo-skin rowing gloves, a donation from Kakadu, an Australian sponsor. I put my oars in the oarlocks and closed the oarlock gates to hold them in place, taking my time and tightening the nut securely. At my word, Astrid cast off the lines and pushed me away from the pontoon. As my boat drifted out between the lines of moored yachts, I strapped

my feet onto the footplate and grasped the textured rubber grips
of the oars. I took a deep breath to gather myself, swung forward
on my sliding seat, placed my blades in the water, and drew cleanly
through to the finish of the stroke—legs, body, and arms coordi-
nating in the familiar motion. My imagination briefly flickered
forward to the many miles that lay ahead and I felt dizzy with the
thought that this was the first stroke of about a million I would
take between here and Antigua.

I paddled slowly and carefully along the alley of moored yachts,
trying not to hit anything, blowing my breath out through my
pursed lips to try and keep myself calm. Rowers sit facing backward, so I had to keep craning my neck around to see where I was
going. As well as watching out for my bows, I had to keep glancing
up to make sure that the array of antennae on the roof of my cabin
didn't collide with any overhanging bowsprits, the long spars that
extend from the bows of sailing boats at a perfect height to ambush
passing ocean rowboats. I slowed down as I approached the end
of the avenue of boats and stuck one blade hard into the water
to pivot myself around the corner. Once I had turned through
ninety degrees I started rowing slowly again, along an even nar-
rower channel that would take me out of the marina. People on
their yachts, some of the voices familiar from the last few days,
called out to wish me luck. I smiled and called back, thanking
them for their good wishes. Distracted, I wasn't paying attention
to where I was going. Too late I saw a yacht's long bowsprit pro-
jecting out over the water. I clunked it with the tall thin rod of my
radar enhancer (an electronic device for making me show up more
clearly on the radar of any passing ships) and swore at myself for
being so clumsy. Mr. Self-Critical joined Mr. Self-Doubt among
the negative voices in my head.

I made it out of the marina and into the harbor, where the
other boats were already waiting. I checked my watch. Still a few

minutes to go. Other rowboats were nearby, and that gave me a fragile sense of security. I fussed around, making a few last-minute adjustments to the footplate. This was my steering mechanism, and I was supposed to be able to lock it into a neutral position when I wanted to go straight, but the lock refused to hold fast. I had wedged a block of wood under the footplate so I could hold a steady course, but it kept shifting under the pressure of my foot. If only I'd had time for more sea trials, I thought ruefully, but time had run out and now I just had to go with what I had.

I looked up from my fidgeting to find that the other boats had moved off toward the start line. The race hadn't even begun, and already I was getting left behind. Fighting to quell my rising anxiety, I paddled hard, trying to catch up. The crew of a passing yacht sounded their horn and wished me bon voyage. They, too, were heading west. "See you in Antigua," I called cheerily, trying to fill my voice with a confidence that was rapidly evaporating.

The starting horn sounded from the Woodvale yacht. The Atlantic Rowing Race 2005 had begun. And I wasn't yet at the starting line. The other crews were racing off and leaving me behind. "Calm down," I tried to convince myself. "You've got three thousand miles to go. A hundred yards now isn't going to make any difference."

But there was an urgency to my paddling as I rowed south out of the harbor and turned west along the coastline, my bow now pointing toward my far-distant destination. I looked over my shoulder to see where the other boats were, but all I could see was a row of rapidly receding dots on the horizon, almost lost in the glare of the bright sunshine ricocheting harshly off the wind-ruffled water. The videotape would show me rowing strongly, looking focused and determined, but inside I felt panicked and nervous. This was it. This was really it. From now on, it was just me, *Sedna*, and the ocean.

....

The day was warm and I was soon covered in a sheen of sweat. The waves were getting bouncier outside the harbor, and I grew hot and uncomfortable. I was already looking forward to my first break from rowing.

After about an hour I decided to stop and try out the water-maker. I stowed the oars and opened the hatch below my rowing seat. I turned the black pressure dial to low pressure for the initial run-through, according to the instructions I had received just that morning. Had I turned it enough? I wasn't sure. I reached into my cabin to switch on the watermaker's power supply at the control panel. The red light came on to show that the electricity was flow-ing. The machine whirred loudly for five seconds and then stopped. Damn.

I turned off the power supply and turned it back on again. Nothing. I adjusted the pressure valve and tried again. Still nothing.

This couldn't be happening. Surely not so early on in the race. After all my preparations and all my training and all my hard work, I couldn't be out of the race almost before it had started. Was this going to be the shortest ocean row ever? The panic and humilia-tion began to rise.

I fiddled around some more, trying to coax the machine into life. The water was getting rougher, and I was starting to feel queasy with seasickness. This was not good timing. I had more important matters on my mind. I needed to get this watermaker working, or my Atlantic attempt would be over. The anxiety swelled in my chest, but I tried to push it back down so I could think straight. What would a *real* adventurer do in this situation? I pulled out the instruction manual and consulted the troubleshooting guide, but rapidly eliminated all possible causes of the problem. Why do troubleshooting guides *never* cover the particular problem that you have? Just whose troubles are they trying to shoot? Not mine, that was for sure. I cursed all writers of technical manuals, and cursed myself for not being more technically competent.

I realized I was going to have to ask for help, embarrassing as that might be, and reluctantly decided to call one of the support yachts. These two sailing boats would accompany the race for its full duration and would be the first people to contact with any problems. They may not be in a position to help directly—they had to support twenty-six boats scattered across half an ocean, so they could be up to a week's sail away—but they were contactable twenty-four hours a day, seven days a week, either by VHF (very high frequency) marine radio, if they were nearby, or by satellite phone, in the more likely event that they were outside the very limited range of the VHF.

Right now they would still be within the range of the VHF—as would all the other crews, who would no doubt witness my embarrassing confession that, just one hour into the race, I was already having to ask for help. Reluctantly I picked up the handset from its cradle on the control panel, and almost whispering in the ridiculous hope that nobody else would hear me, I issued a call on the open race channel.

"This is *Sedna Solo, Sedna Solo, Sedna Solo,* calling *Aurora, Aurora, Aurora.* Come in *Aurora.* Over."

After a moment's pause, "*Sedna Solo,* this is *Aurora.* What can we do for you? Over."

"My watermaker seems not to be working. It used to work, but we changed a filter on it this morning, and now nothing is happening. Any ideas?"

A moment of silence, during which I imagined the crew of the *Aurora* rolling on the deck with helpless laughter at my incompetence. Mr. Self-Critical was having a field day in my head.

"Have you checked that the power supply is turned on?"

"Yes." Give me a break. I may not be technical, but I had at least thought to check that.

"And the water valve is open?"

"Yes."

"Roz, this is George." A familiar voice butted into the conversation. George was a member of one of the two men's fours competing in the race and had become a good friend over the previous summer when we had spent time together during the weeklong Henley Royal Regatta. He had rowed alongside me on a rowing simulator in the pouring rain of an English summer's day while I attempted to raise sponsorship for my race entry fee.

Uh-oh. If George was listening, then probably most of the other competitors had also heard my pathetic plea for help. They'd all know I was a helpless female, having to call for assistance. Great.

"Hiya, George. This is rather embarrassing. I'm having a bit of bother with my watermaker."

"So I heard. I've got an idea. It might be that you've got a big air bubble in the system because of changing that filter. You might need to prime it. Try unscrewing the filter and fill it up with water, then put it back on and try again."

"Oh, OK. I'll give that a go. Thanks."

I hung up the VHF radio mouthpiece and went back out into the cockpit to the watermaker hatch. Unscrew the filter, he'd said. Right.

The filter sat in a clear plastic cylindrical cup, closed at the bottom and fitting into the watermaker system at the top, so that it hung down from its fitting. It had been screwed in tightly by the company rep, and it was a struggle to undo it, especially as my boat was tipping from side to side on the waves and my nausea was increasing by the minute. After a struggle I managed to get it undone and filled the cylindrical cup with water from a jerry can. Then I had to screw it back on. This was much harder.

It was fiddly to get the thread of the screw aligned correctly. I was crouching on the deck of my boat, bottom up, head down in the small hatch, trying to line up the thread on the filter cup. The boat was pitching and my stomach was lurching. Each time I nearly got it lined up, the boat would tip and I would cross-thread the alignment.

And at the back of my mind was an image like an aerial view of La Gomera, an image of the other crews pulling away from me while I wasted time, messing around with my watermaker with my ass in the air. "You're getting left behind, you loser." A new voice— hello, Mr. Competitive.

At last I succeeded. I raised my head out of the hatch with relief, gulping down the fresh air to suppress the rising bile. I reached into the cabin and hit the on button on the control panel. The watermaker whirred into life. Relief surged through me. My race wasn't over yet.

I got back on the VHF radio. "George, you're a genius. That's working great now. Thank you."

"Hey, any time, Savage," he said affectionately. "You take care."

"I certainly will. You too. Bon voyage."

We signed off, and I went back to my rowing seat. The other boats had disappeared from view as our various courses and speeds scattered the crews across the blue sparkling waters of the Atlantic. La Gomera still loomed large as I faced backward in my boat, ply-ing the oars. El Hierro, the last island between here and Antigua, lay ahead, and beyond that nothing but open ocean. I was rowing hard but seemed to be moving at a painfully slow pace, the land slipping by almost imperceptibly. I still felt panicky and unsettled, my thoughts racing. The rapidity of my thoughts contrasted cru-elly with the slowness of my progress. I plowed on.

. . . .

Sunset that day found me hanging over the side of my boat, vomiting into the darkening waters of the Atlantic. Waves of nausea passed through me as seasickness gripped my stomach and ejected its contents. The wind had picked up, whipping the sea into a belly-churning chop. Seasickness and the day's early start were conspiring against me and I was exhausted.

I knew from my limited sailing experience—three voyages adding up to about six weeks on the open ocean—that my seasickness usually passed in a couple of days, during which time I would feel like a wrung-out dishcloth—floppy and gray and disgusting. I had hoped to get farther from land before taking a rest, but now the overwhelming temptation was to lie in my cabin and sleep until I felt better. I fought the nausea and the tiredness for another half an hour, then gave in and decided to retire for the night. With a heavy sigh I brought the oars to a halt, unlocked the oarlocks, and stowed the oars along the gunwales. I peeled off my rowing gloves, stretched out my aching muscles, and made my way over to the cabin hatch in a crouched walk, hanging onto the spare oars for stability on the pitching platform of the deck. Just before I went inside, I stood upright in front of the cabin, my legs straddling the central footwell. I gazed out across the bow of my boat toward the west, where the sun had just dipped down below the rolling waves. Antigua was over there somewhere, three thousand miles away. *Three thousand miles!* How many had I done so far? About twelve. This was going to take forever. One day down, how many still to go? Too many, if they were all going to feel like this. I hung my head and retreated to the cabin, defeated. I felt very small and very alone.

....

Despite my exhaustion I couldn't get to sleep. I kept imagining I was about to be run down by a ship. This may seem unlikely—that in the overall vastness of the Atlantic a large ship and a rowboat could end up occupying exactly the same patch of ocean—but a pair of British men rowing across the North Pacific had been run down by a fishing boat a few years before. It had sliced their boat in half but at least had the decency to stop and pick them up. For these first few days of the race I would be close to shipping lanes, and although the risk was small, it was a risk nonetheless and not conducive to a good night's sleep.

It was noisy in the cabin, too. Like an echo chamber the carbon fiber hull amplified the noise of the waves. Every few minutes a particularly large wave would come along and slam deafeningly into the side of the boat, and I would be sent rolling across my bunk. I was convinced that the rudder pintles could not possibly withstand such violent blows and curled up into a small bundle of anxiety, flinching at every big wave and bracing myself for imminent disaster.

I had set myself a rowing schedule of three hours on, three hours off, so twice during the chilly night I had to haul myself reluctantly off my bunk to return to the oars for a rowing shift and to throw up. Both body and mind protested at this unnatural disruption to their rest, and the hours dragged by. The three-hour rest periods were not much better. I tossed and turned nervously in my bunk, trying and failing to get comfortable on a constantly pitching bed. The huge gulf between my naïve expectations and the brutal reality was beginning to become apparent, and my thoughts were spiraling into negativity. The hostile voices in my head were running riot and telling me what a fool I was for having got myself into this situation.

Mr. Self-Doubt's sneering, insistent little voice was nagging at me, "What the hell do you think you're doing? You're not up to the challenge. You're not tough enough or big enough or strong enough. You did well to get this far. Now quit before it's too late."

I'd been trying to ignore him ever since he'd first piped up earlier in the day, but now I turned my attention on him. "Well, hello again, Self-Doubt," I thought. "I wondered where you'd been these last few years. I thought I'd left you behind, along with my old life, but you seem to have caught up with me again. Who invited you on board?"

So this was the start of my Atlantic Rowing Race. I was at the back of the pack, I was still cringing with embarrassment over the watermaker incident, and now I was wracked with seasickness and doubts and was too scared to sleep. This was not the auspicious start I had been hoping for. It was time to do or die, and right now I didn't feel too confident about which way it was going to go.

three

BEGINNINGS

S elf-Doubt did have a point. His words had penetrated my fragile veneer of self-belief and wormed their way into my mind as I tried to sleep. The nagging question ran through my head again and again—can I do this? Can I do this? It gnawed away at the cheery optimism I had felt before the race. I rummaged back through my past in search of evidence that I could indeed do this, but came up empty-handed. In fact, I decided, if you wanted to recruit an adventurer you would reject my résumé immediately.

As a child I was far from what anyone would call a tomboy. I was timid physically and socially, the teacher's pet, the gawky kid in strange clothes who always had her nose in a book.

I was born in Cheshire, England, on December 23, 1967, which makes me a Capricorn, the mountain goat, supposedly ambitious and determined with an ability to overcome obstacles in pursuit of my goals. Capricorns are restless spirits, always striving to be better tomorrow than they are today, which does not make for a life of easy contentment.

Even if the stars had not already decreed it, my upbringing would have engendered a hunger for self-improvement. My parents were both Methodist preachers, neither of whom had been to university due to family circumstances—my mother had lost her mother at the age of thirteen, and by coincidence my father had lost his father at the same age—so they had both been needed at home to help run the household and the family business, respectively. Possibly because of missing out on higher education in their own lives, they were academically ambitious for me and my sister, Tanya, who was born exactly seventeen months after me. We grew up in a series of provincial English towns as my parents moved from one church appointment to another.

My mother taught Tanya and me to read before we started at school, and with this flying start we were both successful academically, but I lagged far behind my classmates on the athletic field. Because of my academic ability I had been pushed up a grade, so I was by far the youngest and smallest among my peers and was usually the last to be picked on any team.

Only a couple of stories from my childhood give the slightest hint of what was to come several decades later. In the first story, my family was on holiday at Filey, on the east coast of Yorkshire, when I was about eighteen months old. One day on the beach I decided that I wanted to go for a walk. I wanted to go alone, and apparently made this quite plain. Wearing only a diaper, I set out along the sand, as single-minded and purposeful as only a young child with a mission can be. My mother followed at a discreet distance, and since there were quite a number of people on the beach it was not difficult for her to remain out of sight as she tailed her determined daughter.

I had toddled along for about a quarter of a mile when I stopped to pick up a shell. I was standing still, admiring it, when Mum approached me and suggested we go back. I refused. But Mum figured out a way to talk me out of my intrepid adventure. She suggested that I should go and show Daddy the shell that I had found. Always eager for an opportunity to please my father, I abandoned my expedition and trotted happily back along the beach to where he, my grandma, and Tanya were waiting. But only my mother's timely intervention had stopped me in my attempt to become the first toddler ever to totter all the way to Scotland.

The second story, as my mother tells it, took place when I was about seven years old. A sponsored run was being held on the sports field of a local school to raise funds for a charity. I had not been well—I had been suffering from scarlet fever, an extreme form of strep throat that causes a rash—and my mother would not allow me to do more than one lap of the field. I was disappointed at not being allowed to complete the distance, and the following weekend my father took me back to have another go, to prove to myself that I could have done a full mile. I did the mile and a bit more, to my immense satisfaction—and no doubt that of my father, who always encouraged me to push myself just a little harder, although never as relentlessly as he pushed himself. Through his example, coupled with my desire to win his approval, I absorbed the lesson that to strive for success was the way things should be.

....

My father's quarterly stipend was small, so despite my mother's careful housekeeping, our Sunday dinner would deteriorate from roast chicken at the start of the quarter to cheap beef meatballs by the end. The family finances didn't stretch to many store-bought clothes, so my sister and I wore dresses made by my mother on her old-fashioned hand-cranked sewing machine, and cardigans knitted by kindly church members. At school our homemade clothes marked us out as different, as did our accents, which always took a year or so to conform to the local norm as we moved around the country. Being perceived as "brainy," usually a term of derision, differentiated us further. I used to yearn to be just like everybody else, to have a nice normal name, like "Jane Smith" or "Amanda Jones," instead of my clunky moniker of Rosalind Savage. But it seemed to be my lot in life to be the perpetual outsider, never quite accepted as part of the gang.

Books were my escape and my refuge. Books did not judge me or call me names, and they allowed me to escape temporarily from my awkward reality into the wonderful world of my imagination. In the house where we lived while I was ages two to seven, my second-floor bedroom had a small, triangular bay window, which jutted out from the wall of the upper story. To me it seemed like my enchanted tower, my special sanctuary. I would curl myself up on the windowsill and sit there for hours at a time, devouring books by Enid Blyton—the Famous Five and Secret Seven series—about groups of friends who went on adventures involving caves and tunnels and explorations. I fantasized about having adventures of my own, but I was quite content to live out the fantasies in my mind, being an indoorsy, introspective kind of child.

That night on the ocean, I smiled ruefully as I rowed along under the starlit sky, thinking about my former child self. Rowing across an ocean is just the kind of story that would have appealed to me when I was a little girl. In my imagination it would have seemed such a romantic adventure—the solitary voyager, making a pilgrim's progress across the big blue ocean while dolphins and mermaids frolicked alongside the boat and seabirds swooped and sang overhead. Now that I was here, living it for real, it seemed anything but romantic. So far it had been rather cold, uncomfortable, and nauseating. But this was good—thinking about my childhood was distracting me from the present—so I allowed my mind's eye to wander back to the past.

....

When I was an impressionable sixteen, in 1984, we went abroad as a family for the first time—to the United States. That summer would have a fundamental impact on how I saw myself, and how I saw my future.

Our trip to San Diego was the result of a program that facilitated travel exchanges between Methodist ministers. My father would spend six weeks looking after a church in the wealthy suburb of La Mesa while we lived in their minister's house, and the American minister and his wife would swap into my father's posting in Cambridge, England. Members of Foothills Methodist Church enthusiastically embraced this family of British visitors. They treated us to visits to Disneyland, the Grand Canyon, and Mexico. We went with the church youngsters in an old school bus to the beach at La Jolla, and to pool parties where we would hop from hot tub to swimming pool and eat chocolate brownies until we felt sick.

We were taken out to restaurants and ice cream parlors. As I sat in my rowing seat I salivated as I remembered the Big Olafs—a huge sugar cone stacked full of as many flavors of ice cream as could fit, drenched in chocolate sauce and sprinkled with nuts. Seasickness aside, I would have given almost anything for a Big Olaf right now. Back home in England we never ate out because we couldn't afford it. I had never before seen a swimming pool in somebody's backyard, nor a house with more than one bathroom. The standard of living in San Diego was unlike anything I had ever imagined. Life there seemed so much better than our life back home, with our secondhand clothes and cheap cuts of meat. I soaked up the lifestyle along with the sunshine. Now I had seen how the other half lived, and I wanted to live that way, too. I wanted money, a big house, and beautiful possessions. Surely, I thought, these things would make me happy.

If that summer introduced me to materialism, it also showed me the Californian way to personal reinvention that would ultimately make me question those same materialistic values. It started off in a small way as a by-product of an obsession with my weight—I started collecting the nutrition leaflets available in San Diego supermarkets. I progressed to reading books on diet and exercise written by American models and actresses. From there I graduated to reading about broader concepts of self-improvement, psychological as well as physical. I eased off on the ice cream and developed a voracious appetite for self-help books instead. I was introduced to the notion that I could be whatever and whoever I wanted to be. Too fat? Diet! Not fit? Exercise! Not happy? Change! Take control! Choose your destiny!

It was the start of my belief that I was not merely a creation of my genes, star sign, upbringing, or circumstances. I, and I alone, had responsibility for my life. I could do with it as I chose. The problem was, I had no idea what to choose. It would take me another two decades to figure that one out.

....

The winter after we returned from San Diego, I won a place at the prestigious University of Oxford—to this day, I know not how. I suspected an administrative error, but decided to go along with the good fortune that fate had chosen to bestow on me. My parents, of course, were delighted and proud.

I had decided that this would be a good opportunity to take up a sport. At school I hated physical education—it wasn't the exercise I loathed so much as the showers. Besides being the youngest in my year, I was also a late physical developer, so I was the last girl in my class to start wearing a bra. Communal changing rooms and shared showers were an excruciating embarrassment to me. I was ashamed of my body and didn't want anyone to see my lack of physical maturity. I even took up an extra academic subject, Latin, to avoid half the week's physical education lessons, and was much happier in the classroom than on the sports field.

Throughout my teens I had struggled with my weight. My appetite was, and still is, too big for my body. I constantly want to consume quantities way beyond what my body can burn. One reason that rowing the Atlantic had appealed to me was that I would be burning around five thousand calories a day, so for once in my life I would be able to eat as much as I wanted without gaining weight. I'd overlooked the fact that although I could eat as *much* as I wanted, I would not be able to eat *what* I wanted. Yes, sure I could pig out . . . on freeze-dried expedition meals and prepackaged snack bars. Life has a cruel sense of irony.

At the age of fourteen I had embarked on an almost constant round of diets—meal replacements, Weight Watchers, counting calories—but the effects rarely lasted. I had once successfully lost nearly twenty pounds in six weeks with Weight Watchers, only to regain it all, and then some, in the six weeks that followed. When I went to an all-girls school for my final two years before university, weight watching became a major preoccupation as my friends and I became competitive dieters, seeing who could bring in the tiniest packed lunch. Eating disorders were common, and obsessions with food and body weight almost universal.

I knew there had to be a better way. Physical exertion appealed no more at the age of eighteen than it had done at school, but I was tired of the self-control needed to control my weight purely through dieting, and I knew that exercise would allow me to eat

more without getting fat. If the three options were self-depriva-
tion, obesity, or exercise, exercise seemed to be the least of the evils.

Rowing appealed because few girls would have rowed before,
unlike any of the other sports more commonly taught at school
level, so my prior lack of sporting success would be less of a hand-
icap. I took to rowing with all the zeal of the convert, and the
captain of the women's rowing club encouraged me in my newfound passion. Soon I was rowing with the college women's First
Eight, and I delighted in finally having found a sport where I got
picked first rather than last, which had always been my fate in
lower school games.

My confidence grew, and in my second year at university my
rowing career got a lucky break. The Oxford University women's
squad had fallen into disarray, and they were in dire need of fresh
trialists. Oxford University is comprised of thirty-nine colleges,
each college being a community of roughly three hundred students
studying a wide cross-section of subjects. The best sportsmen and
sportswomen from each college vie for selection to the university teams to compete in the annual events against Oxford's old
rival, the University of Cambridge. In 1987, the Oxford women's
head coach had quit, and a large number of rowers had walked
out in sympathy. The new coaches were desperate for women to
try out for selection. I was in the right place at the right time, and
despite being a good few inches too short to be a heavyweight
rower I squeaked into the number two seat in the heavyweight
reserve crew. I won my first half-blue by racing against Cambridge
at Henley in March 1988.

I decided I wanted to row for the university lightweights crew
the upcoming year. To win selection I would have to lose ten
pounds and get more fit than I had ever been in my life. I trained
and dieted throughout that summer. I put together a training
program and diet plan and followed it religiously. While at home

during the vacation I had limited access to equipment, but I ran and cycled and did body circuits, using my body weight as resistance for a punishing series of squats, jumps, push-ups, sit-ups, and crunches. I sweated off the pounds one by one, and I returned to Oxford lighter and stronger and very determined.

My dedication paid off, and to my immense satisfaction, I was selected to the stroke seat, arguably the most prestigious seat in the boat. The stroke's main job is to set the rhythm for the rest of the crew—and in rowing, rhythm is everything. When the whole crew is moving in unison to an efficient rhythm, powerful through the water and relaxed on the recovery, the boat feels like it is flying. I felt I was ready for the responsibility. I was on course for my second half-blue, I was in the stroke seat, and I was ecstatic. The morning after the crew was announced I woke up feeling better than I had ever felt before. I looked in the bathroom mirror and smiled at myself—smiled at the future stroke of the Oxford University Women's Lightweight Eight. For the first time in my life, I had set my heart on a goal because it was what I wanted to do, rather than because it was what someone else wanted or expected me to do, and through my own hard work I had achieved it. The sense of accomplishment was huge.

But after university, rowing succumbed to the pressures of adult life. I continued rowing for five years after I started work in London, but struggled to fit the training around fourteen-hour days in the office. I never again reached the heights of my Oxford rowing career, losing out in trials to taller, heavier women. No matter how hard I trained or how much I ate, I would never get any bigger—wider, very likely, but no taller. I heard just once too often from a rowing coach, "a good big'un will always beat a good littl'un," and retired from the sport.

I would occasionally get a pang of nostalgia when I saw a crew out on the River Thames on a summer's morning, their bodies moving in unison, a neat pattern of ripples spreading out from the dips of their oars. I missed the camaraderie of a crew, and the intense mental focus that came from rowing every stroke to the best of my ability. I would have to remind myself of how crushed I'd felt by my final deselection and consider myself lucky to be out of the rowing scene. It would be ten years before I would hold an oar again, and that would be to compete in the Atlantic Rowing Race.

four

WHAT WAS I THINKING?

*d*ay two of the Atlantic Rowing Race dawned clear and sunny. I was woken by a beam of sunlight shafting across my eyelids like a searchlight as the boat rocked on the waves. Eventually I had become too exhausted to worry any more and managed to get a couple of hours of sleep during my last rest shift. I took a physical inventory of my body. I was relieved to find that my seasickness had abated slightly, but I had woken up with a worrying ache in my ribs. When I'd been struggling with the watermaker the day before I'd leaned across my knee to reach something and had felt a sudden pain in the side of my ribcage, so I'd probably pulled a muscle. This was a cause for concern—there would be no recovery time. I had to get back to the oars. But the brightness of the day helped to banish the demons that had haunted the night, and overall I was starting to feel more positive.

My appetite never disappears for long—more's the pity. I hadn't eaten much the day before and I was hungry so I set about making a breakfast of tea and porridge. Although I had practiced the procedure a number of times on dry land, the prospect of using the camping stove apparatus on the open sea made me anxious.

Highly flammable liquid fuel combined with an erratically tipping rowboat seemed a potential recipe for disaster.

I reached into my cabin, undid a couple of latches, and lifted out a section of the floor. Fixed to the underside of this panel was a nine-inch-high stainless-steel cylinder that would act as a windbreak. A camping stove was mounted to the board inside it. A flexible tube led from the camping stove to a pressurized fuel bottle, which was also fixed to the panel. To use the stove I inverted the whole assembly so that the panel formed a base with the cylinder on top, and secured the panel outside in the cockpit using a couple of swivel latches. Peering in through a viewing hole in the side of the metal cylinder, I pumped the plunger into the fuel bottle to create the necessary pressure, turned the valve to allow a teaspoonful of fuel to dribble into the top of the burner, and lit it with a barbecue lighter. Big yellow flames immediately erupted from the stove. This was exactly as it was supposed to work but the flickering flames leaped alarmingly from the top of the protective metal cylinder and I quickly pulled my long hair back out of the way to prevent it from catching fire. When the yellow flames subsided I turned the valve to change the flame from flickering yellow to high-pressure blue so I could start cooking.

I turned the valve too far and the flame went out, starved of fuel.

"Bugger." I swore out loud.

This was not supposed to happen, but even in practice on dry land it had done so with annoying regularity. Now I would have to wait for the apparatus to cool down before I could try again. If I tried it too soon, the residual heat would cause the fuel to evaporate before I had time to light it.

At the second attempt I got the stove fired up and put the kettle on to boil. In just a few minutes it was steaming away and I used an oven cloth to lift it and poured the boiling water into a wide-mouth thermos, over the instant porridge I had already put in there. I gave the mixture a good stir and then put the lid on to allow the porridge to "cook." It was supposed to be cooked over heat while stirring, but a sticky porridge pan was too much trouble to wash up, and I'd found through experimentation that the porridge would absorb the water quite adequately if I left it to sit in the thermos for a while. I put the remainder of the hot water into a larger thermos to be used later for hot drinks and to rehydrate my dinner. After waiting ten minutes I opened up the thermos of porridge and added dried fruit and ground cinnamon and ginger, stirring them into the gooey porridge mixture.

"Mmmm. Yummy." I sat on the deck by the hatch to the aft sleeping cabin, my feet in the footwell, and spooned the hot food into my mouth, relishing the comforting sensation as it warmed my core and restored my blood sugar levels. I immediately started to feel better. I congratulated myself on managing to prepare breakfast without setting fire to either the boat or myself, and decided that maybe the ocean wasn't such a bad place after all. Maybe I could even begin to feel at home here. I needed to start focusing on the positive aspects of my experience, rather than the negative. This one small victory helped restore my sense of self-belief, which had taken such a knocking the night before. As I ate I looked out across the waves, sparkling in the morning sunlight. I wondered where the other crews were, and how they had fared during their first night at sea.

I looked over at the Argos locator beacon, blinking its red light in the corner of the cockpit behind my rowing position. It was sending a message from my boat that would bounce off a network of satellites orbiting the earth to a central control center in France. Each of the boats in the race had been equipped with one of these, so the race organizers and anybody checking the race website would be able to see the latitude and longitude of every crew.

I knew that Mum would be anxiously watching the little purple blob that represented *Sedna* and me, as we edged our way slowly across the online map of the Atlantic. It made me feel irrationally safer to know that she was watching over me. I made believe that the red blinking light of the Argos was beaming a slender umbilical cord through the ether, from me to my mother, and found the thought reassuring.

I scraped the last of the porridge out of the thermos, savoring every last dollop, washed up using a little hot water from the large thermos, and returned the camping stove to its stowed position inside the cabin. I was just about to start my day's rowing when I spotted a white sail wending its way across the waves toward me. As the sail came closer I could see it was attached to a vessel—the support yacht *Aurora*.

I had not seen the yacht, nor indeed any of the rowboats, since they had disappeared into the distance while I was struggling with the watermaker. During my preparations for the row some people had seemed disappointed to hear that I would be a competitor in a race, rather than going totally solo. They seemed to imagine that I would be in a little flotilla of boats rowing together across the Atlantic, chatting and laughing and comparing notes at the end of each day. There was also a misconception that the support yachts would be constantly on hand to provide tea, sympathy, and home-cooked food. The truth was that I would be very unlikely to see any of the other competitors, and the support yachts would be there for me only if I chose to contact them, and even then they could be up to a week away. But I did not plan to make contact, for I was afraid that if I started an ongoing dialogue with them I would fail in one of the key tasks I had set myself: to assert my independence and self-sufficiency, and to find out what I could do when cast entirely on my own means.

I had spent most of my life relying on other people for support—my parents, teachers, boyfriends, and my husband—and now I wanted to find out if I was strong enough and resourceful enough to survive alone. I was tired of having to rely on other people, for a few disappointments had taught me that I could truly rely on nobody but myself. Within the last couple of years I had some grand schemes that had depended on other people to provide something—the financing for a coffee shop, a boat for a trip around the world, the premises for a baking business—and in every case the plans had fallen apart. It had been nobody's fault, but circumstances change, as do people's priorities, and each of these promises of support had failed to materialize. More recently, the drive to raise corporate sponsorship for my row had been one letdown after another—promises implied, only to be told, "Sorry, we've had budget cuts," or "There's been a change of strategy." As for men, in no other area of my life was it more true that hope had given way to disappointment. In my headlong, headstrong way I had tended to throw myself wholeheartedly into relationships, with giddy expectations unfounded in reality, only to suffer disillusionment and pain when the honeymoon period ended and the violins of romance trailed off into discord and then embarrassed silence.

My lifelong tendency to rely on others meant that my repertoire of practical skills was sadly limited, and although I suspected that I was capable of more than I imagined, in ordinary life the temptation to take the easy option and ask for help was too much for me to resist. The only way that I could resist the temptation was to remove myself from it—so one of the reasons that rowing the Atlantic had appealed was that it would be the perfect way to effectively cut myself off from any hope of assistance. I would be forced to fend for myself. A blunt-speaking Australian oar maker had summed it up when we had been talking at Henley Regatta the summer before. "You women," he'd said. "I know what you're like. You flutter your eyelashes and you get someone else to do the dirty work for you. You're going to have to stop fluttering the eyelashes and start doing things for yourself if you're going to survive out there on the ocean."

So this was my goal: if I could get myself from the Canaries to Antigua, alone and unsupported, I would have passed my self-imposed test of self-sufficiency. This meant that I felt very protective about my solitude, and did not welcome intrusions. The less contact I had with the outside world, the better—I did not want to be tempted into relying on anyone else for support. For better or worse, right or wrong, this was *my* adventure and I would do it my way.

The sleek white craft pulled alongside and the skipper, Lin Barker, called me on the VHF radio to ask how I was doing. The truth was that after my hearty breakfast I was once again feeling nauseous from the motion of the boat, and the discomfort in my ribs was bothering me, but I assured Lin I was doing just fine. I didn't want them fussing over me.

I asked for an update on the other competitors. I wanted to know how my progress compared with theirs. "You're not coming last, but most of the crews are ahead of you," Lin told me. "You're doing just fine, especially as you're the only solo woman."

But I wanted to do better than "just fine." I wanted to be a contender.

"You need to row more hours in the day," declared Mr. Competitive, smugly. "I know," I shot back, through gritted teeth. "But my ribs hurt and I feel seasick, so it will just have to wait until I feel better. There are still plenty of miles ahead for me to catch up with the rest, so there's no need to panic." Mr. Competitive gave me a superior, you-know-I'm-right kind of a look.

After five or so minutes of chatting with Lin on the VHF radio, I was getting impatient to get on with rowing, so I signed off. The *Aurora* turned to allow the wind to fill her sails and took off with enviable speed to visit the other crews ahead of me.

I returned to my rowing seat and took up the oars once more. Slide, dip, draw, finish. Slide, dip, draw, finish. Stroke after stroke after stroke. Stop for a drink of water every fifteen minutes. Stop for a five-minute snack break every hour. Stop for a longer rest every three hours.

I had worked hard to train my muscles for this, but despite the rigorous training program of the last fourteen months my body already seemed to be cracking under the pressure. As well as the persistent pain in my ribs, I was developing an ominous grinding pain in my shoulders that I knew from my Oxford rowing days indicated the onset of tendinitis, an inflammation of the tendons that should be treated with rest and the regular application of ice. Neither rest nor ice were options right now. I winced with every stroke, as the pain between my shoulder blades increased as the day wore on.

I felt indignant. This was not fair! I had, as far as I knew, trained longer and harder than any other ocean rower ever had. I had built up a solid base of fitness by training for between one and four hours a day—lifting weights, running, and training on a rowing machine—until my schedule eventually peaked with weekly sixteen-hour rowing sessions, split into four shifts of four hours. I would start at noon on a Sunday and finish around dawn on Monday morning. These sessions had been tough. Physically, my lower back would be aching and my body protesting that it wanted sleep. Psychologically, I fought boredom and mental fatigue, training my mind to entertain itself while my body rowed on through the night. I passed the time listening to music and visualizing what life would be like on the ocean. At last the sixteen hours of rowing would draw to an end and I would collapse gratefully off the rowing machine, drained and sweating, but proud of my perseverance and growing in confidence that I could rise to the physical challenge of rowing an ocean.

But now I was starting to wonder if all those hours spent in training had been a waste of time. The whole point had been to prepare my body for this kind of punishing rowing schedule, but the movement on the rowing machine had been comfortable, regular, forward and backward, which was ideal for rowers intending to compete on smooth waters but was poor preparation for the ocean. Out here the water was choppy, the boat tipped from side to side, and my oars rarely made a solid connection with the water—or at least not simultaneously. It seemed that my eight years of rowing experience would be of little use to me now. On the flat, calm rivers where I had spent most of my rowing career, I had been able to compensate for my lack of size by rowing with a sharp, precise technique that moved the boat efficiently through the water. In response to the rough water and large, heavy boat, I was now developing an odd, syncopated rowing rhythm. My rowing coaches would not have been proud. Ideally I would have done more of my training in the boat, rather than on the rowing machine, but the boat had not been ready in time. "If only, if only," I thought regretfully.

As the second day of the Atlantic Rowing Race passed slowly, the seas rose, pounding the oars and sending shock waves traveling up the shaft to my shoulders, until they felt as if I was taking a beating in the boxing ring rather than rowing an ocean. I also found that I was unable to row at full slide as I had done on the rowing machine. In a rowboat the shoes are fixed to a plate so that the rower's feet stay in one place while the rowing seat slides back and forth. This allows the rower to exploit the power of the large quad muscles in their legs as well as the smaller muscles of their upper body. But I was finding that the rougher the water, the less of the slide I could use, so most of the power of the stroke was coming from my relatively weak arms and shoulders rather than my stronger, fitter thigh muscles.

I had believed that with my fitness, determination, and sleek new carbon fiber boat, I might succeed in my objective of not coming in last—but my strategy hinged on spending sixteen hours per day at the oars. This goal was undoubtedly ambitious. Most of the competing crews were pairs, and would row in alternating shifts of two hours on, two hours off, making a total of twelve hours apiece in any twenty-four-hour period. I was intending to row a third as much again—on my own.

As I thought about the pairs, just for the briefest of moments I wished I had a crewmate sharing this experience. I wanted to ask, "Am I doing this right? Is it really meant to be this hard?" Having a partner would have had another advantage, too—as a solo rower, while I was sleeping my boat would just drift with the wind and the current, whereas the crews of two or more would always have someone awake and rowing, keeping the boat moving faster and in the right direction. But almost as quickly as those thoughts came, I banished them from my mind. I had good reasons to be doing this alone, and I had to accept that with the advantages would also come some disadvantages.

But no sooner had I banished the negativity from my mind than it surged back again. Could I really do this? In the bustle of preparation there had been no time to stop and ponder this question. All my energy had been focused on getting to the start line, which many people had told me was the hardest part. It had undeniably been challenging, but it had been mostly within my comfort zone. The skills involved were fund raising, training, and project management—all of which I had done before. The actual act of rowing an ocean, on the other hand, was totally new to me. The fact that I had eight years of rowing experience behind me had given me the happy delusion that I was qualified to take on this challenge, but rowing on the River Thames and rowing on the ocean were proving to be as different as climbing the stairs and climbing Mount Everest.

The enormity of the task ahead was starting to dawn on me, and it was not a comfortable feeling. Self-doubt overwhelmed me. What on earth had possessed me to take on this challenge? I must have been crazy. And I had nobody but myself to blame.

five

BARING MY SOUL—AND MORE

*O*n my third day at sea, I got naked. I am usually modest—and since my pre-race weight gain had much to be modest about—and not given to exhibitionism, but it was generally accepted in the ocean rowing community that rowing with no clothes on was the best way to avoid saltwater sores, which can be excruciatingly painful. The theory was that clothes soak up seawater, which evaporates to leave a crust of salt in the fabric that then acts like sandpaper on skin, creating abrasions that are vulnerable to infection. For me, the incentive to try it was because it was easier to apply sun cream without having to work around garments, and because it was difficult to maintain three points of contact with the boat while pulling down my shorts to go to the bathroom.

To my surprise, the sensation of being naked in the open air was healthy and wholesome rather than strange or embarrassing. A safe distance from prying eyes, the sun and wind felt good on my skin, and made me feel more at home in this alien environment. It was as if I had removed a barrier between myself and the ocean, abandoning one of the trappings of civilization and surrendering myself to nature.

In the afternoon I even briefly rediscovered my sense of humor. What else could I do but laugh, when finding myself naked except for hat, trainers, and kangaroo skin gloves, paddling sedately across three thousand miles of ocean and singing along to Abba?

But it was not long before Mr. Self-Doubt appeared again. After the choppy seas of the first two days, the weather turned hot and sticky. There was no wind, and I felt as if I were rowing through treacle. The water was so flat and calm that instead of only seeing as far as the next wave, I could now see as far as the horizon. The ocean seemed utterly terrible and almost frightening in its vastness—endless and infinite, making me feel very small and insignificant by comparison.

During the sailing trips of my preparation phase I had found that my favorite days were those of long, lazy, medium-sized waves, when the seascape reminded me of the rolling hills of rural England. As the boat would reach the top of a wave I could see a series of waves stretching away from me, while from the bottom of a trough I could see only as far as the next wave's crest. The rise and fall of the boat, and the ever-changing view, made the ocean seem almost like a cozy place. Paradoxically I felt protected amid the waves, private in my secluded little nook of the ocean. By contrast, on these scary days of flat calm I felt exposed and vulnerable.

I was also discovering that, although my boat had no sail, the cabins acted as a very significant wind catcher that made a major difference to my speed over the water. While the wind had been blowing briskly I had been making fair progress, but now that the wind had dropped so did my speed, from about two knots to one. A knot is one nautical mile per hour, and a nautical mile is 1.15 miles, so my speed now was equivalent to a very slow walk. It seemed that El Hierro, the westernmost of the Canary Islands, was never going to disappear from sight. I began to suspect it of following me.

I ran the numbers in my head and worked out how long it would take me to get to Antigua at this snail's pace. About eight months. Unimaginable. The math depressed me.

As I slogged along, becalmed, I anxiously watched the red ensign flag hanging limply from the short mast that supported my navigation light. I longed to see it flutter to signal a returning breeze but it sullenly refused to move. My rowing was regularly punctuated by long, despairing sighs as I wondered what I had done to deserve such unhelpful weather, and imagined the other crews opening up an enormous lead over me.

Patience does not come naturally to me, and this slow pace was all the more marked in contrast to the fourteen months of hectic preparation that had led up to the race. My father often used to say, "Whatever you do, put your whole heart into it," and I had learned this lesson well. I tended to focus on a single project almost to the point of obsession, giving it my all in an intense outpouring of energy and dedication. I had rejected the advice of others that I should aim for the 2007 race since I could not possibly be ready in time for the 2005 launch. I had stubbornly insisted that I could get everything together in little over a year, and through my stubbornness and sheer force of will, I had made it happen. But during those fourteen months I had grown used to living life on fast-forward, and in comparison I now seemed to be moving in slow motion. In my imagination I was already picturing the finish line, but in reality I had hardly begun. I wondered if the discrepancy would drive me crazy.

I tried to cheer myself up by reminding myself of the surfers' saying: "A bad day on the water is still better than a good day in the office." Although it was hard to imagine it right now, life could be worse—I could be back in my old life, putting on a suit and getting on a commuter train and going to work in an office tower in the City of London. It may not be nice to rejoice in the misfortune of others, but it cheered me up to think that I was no longer one of the millions of glum-faced people commuting to the office every weekday. For eleven years I had been one of those millions, and I could remember the feeling of deep gloom at getting up in the dark on a cold winter's morning, trudging to the station, and getting on a train full of equally gloomy commuters who were already planning their next vacation to give themselves something to look forward to.

So I might be over two thousand miles from my next hot meal, cold beer, or decent shower, but at least I wasn't straphanging in the overcrowded train carriages of London's Waterloo and City Line, crammed into the armpit of a stranger.

....

My mind's eye turned inward, away from the flat blue ocean and back to my twenty-one-year-old self. I was waking up in a small bedroom in a shared flat in Fulham, London, and getting ready for my first day at work with an international management consultancy. I showered and dressed: a cream blouse, a narrow-fitting black skirt with a fine pinstripe, and a matching fitted jacket. Smart black pumps with a modest heel completed the outfit. I pulled my hair up into a clip and put on a pair of discreet silver earrings. I stood back from the mirror to admire the overall effect, and barely recognized myself. I looked so grown-up. I didn't look like me at all.

It was 1989, and I had just graduated from Oxford. This job was exactly what I had dreamed of—in my first year of work I would earn three times as much as my father's annual stipend. Although I respected my parents for following their vocations into the church, I did not want to live as they had done, struggling to make ends meet and living a life of frugal economy. I wanted money and all it could buy. This was the time of Thatcher's Britain and Reagan's America, when greed was good and lunch was for wimps, to quote the defining movie of the era, *Wall Street*. Everybody wanted to be a management consultant or an investment banker, and so did I. I had thrown myself into what the British call the milk round, an annual frenzy of recruitment activity in which many big companies give presentations at Britain's top universities, wooing students with promises of impressive starting salaries and plying them with free alcohol and food. This time of feast and plenty was followed by the hard grind of job applications and interviews, leading to offers or rejections. As I rode the bus from Oxford into London for job interviews that winter, I would gaze out of the window at the expensive houses and apartments along Holland Park Avenue and dream of the day when my glittering career would afford me this same glamorous lifestyle. I was ecstatic when Andersen Consulting offered me a job as an associate consultant in their Financial Markets Division—I would be earning good money, and I would be meeting the expectations of my peers and my parents. It looked like I was on the fast track to success.

But as I arrived at the Andersen office in Arundel Street— the premises took up most of the block—and pushed my way through the tinted revolving door into the smart but sterile lobby, all white walls and blond wood paneling, I felt like an imposter. As the revolving door whumped gradually to a halt behind me, the voice of Self-Doubt piped up. "What are you doing here? You don't belong. Look at all these smart, professional people. You're just a little girl dressed up in a smart suit. Who are you trying to fool?" I looked over at the receptionists sitting behind the bastion of their desks. They looked intimidating, with their long, polished fingernails and immaculate hair. I passed my hand self-consciously over my head, smoothing my hair back into the plastic hairclip that earlier I had thought looked so sophisticated but now seemed like a child's toy. I took a deep breath and went over to the least scary-looking receptionist to announce myself. This was it. This was the beginning of life as a working adult.

Those early days did little to silence the voice of Self-Doubt. On my return from Andersen Consulting's intensive induction course in Chicago, I was assigned menial tasks around the office while I waited to be assigned to a client project. In consultant acronym-speak, these were known as SLJs (Shitty Little Jobs), but I struggled even with these. I remember one particular incident that even now causes me to blush with embarrassment.

Throughout college all my essays had been written in longhand, and I hadn't touched a computer since doing a small amount of programming at school. That had been in the days when all commands were entered via a keyboard. As far as I knew, a mouse was a small rodent. One of the first tasks I was given was to make some simple amendments to a document using a mouse-based application.

"You click on the file to open it," said the consultant who was supervising me. "Then make the changes I've marked on this hard copy, and click here to save the file. I have to go to a meeting now. I'll be back in an hour to see how you're getting on."

He left me to it. I moved the mouse until the cursor was over the file icon. Click. Nothing happened. I clicked again. Still nothing. I was baffled. I tried clicking slowly and deliberately. I tried clicking quickly. I tried clicking hard. Nothing worked. One hour later, the consultant came back. I confessed that I hadn't even been able to open the file.

"That's strange," he said. He double-clicked on the icon, and the document appeared on the monitor.

"Oh," I said, light dawning. "You have to click twice. Why didn't you say so?"

He looked at me with an expression of amazement and thinly disguised contempt.

"Stupid," muttered Mr. Self-Critical.

My would-be glittering career had got off to a bad start, and I never recovered my confidence. I suspected myself of being what the more senior consultants referred to in yet another acronym as a PURE—a Previously Undetected Recruiting Error. The cruel label stuck in my mind, and even though nobody ever called me that directly, they didn't need to—the voices in my head did all the negative name-calling for them. I knew I wasn't stupid—I had the academic record to prove that—but I seemed unable to get the hang of this strange, grown-up world of work. The fluorescent-lit offices were an alien environment, and the gray blandness of it all depressed my spirit. But I wanted the money and the prestige, so I pushed my doubt aside and got on with it. Everybody else seemed to find it quite normal, and I hoped that eventually I would, too.

One redeeming feature of that stage of my life was the interesting and intelligent people I met through work, one of whom would later become my husband. Richard also worked for Andersen Consulting, and in 1991 we were assigned to the same project in the provincial English town of Milton Keynes. When we first met I thought he was arrogant and overprivileged, but after we had got shamefully drunk together one evening I saw a softer side to him, and soon I was completely smitten. He was tall and handsome, with blond hair and green eyes. He was athletic and charismatic, and if he was intellectually arrogant, he had good reason to be. He was a graduate from Oxford's old rival, Cambridge University, where he had distinguished himself in Latin, Greek, and Ancient History. I had been out with equally good-looking guys before, but never anybody who could match Richard's combination of looks and brains. He had a huge knowledge of music, books, politics, international affairs, history, and geography.

We were close in age and similar in background—both his parents having been school teachers—so we shared a common outlook on life, and both embraced the qualities of hard work, decency, honesty, and reliability. I admired his intelligence, and loved it that he was no highbrow snob—we could be listening to beautiful, elegiac Gregorian chants as we lay together in bed one night, and the next night he might be dancing maniacally with his friends at an AC/DC rock concert. He made me laugh, and I enjoyed spending time with him and his crowd, all of whom welcomed me into their circle. He was generally popular and respected among his peers, and I basked in his reflected glory. Our relationship bolstered my fragile self-esteem—if somebody this special wanted to be with me, then I must be all right. We started living together shortly after we met and were married five years later when I was twenty-eight. There is a photograph of us on our wedding day, framed by the Gothic arched doorway of the church. I am hanging tightly onto Richard's arm, and I am beaming up at him as if I can't believe my good fortune. He is looking down at me with a joyful expression of love and pride. It was the happiest day of our lives, and we believed it was forever.

That had been ten years ago, but as I rowed my little boat under a blue Atlantic sky now fading to dusk, it still seemed almost as if it were yesterday. I suffered a brief pang of longing for those feelings of love and security, and almost wished that Richard were here with me now, to take me in his strong arms and reassure me that everything was going to be okay. But then I shook off the feeling, this relic of the past, and reminded myself sternly that I was on my own now because I chose to be, so that I could grow strong and self-sufficient, needing nobody but myself.

To banish the pang of nostalgia I needed to find a memory of the past that made me glad to have left it behind, so I thought back once again to my so-called career. The management consultancy had followed an up-or-out promotion policy, and when it became clear to my bosses that I lacked the confidence and assertiveness to go up, they suggested I get out. It was an opportunity for me to change direction, but I still didn't know what I wanted to do. Even though I was clearly not in a job that suited me, I had no better ideas, or at least none that would provide me with the sort of income that I had come to regard as necessary. Despite an increasing body of evidence that this kind of work and I were not well matched, I found myself caught in the salary trap. I might hate the work, but it was a means to an end, and that end was money. I moved to an almost identical role in a different company.

After another three years in management consultancy I moved on but not forward, yet again failing to take the opportunity for a radical change. I took on a similar role in an investment bank, knowing even during the interviews that I was feigning enthusiasm for a job I didn't really want to do, but the substantial increase in pay was irresistible.

I had the standard of living I'd thought I wanted, but my quality of life was plummeting. I was spending sixty hours a week in tedious and unproductive committee meetings, slaving late into the night over PowerPoint presentations, pandering to bosses, and tiptoeing through the minefield of office politics. I knew it didn't feel right, but in common with many human beings I had an amazing capacity for self-delusion and doublethinking that enabled me to know something and yet not know it at the same time—because I simply didn't want to know it. Even though I was such a misfit for my job and despised it every hour of the day, it gave me the income to buy the things that I thought would make me happy.

I finished my rowing shift and went into the cabin to write up my logbook and have a rest. I had decided that three hours on, three hours off, twenty-four hours a day, was too tough, so I was experimenting with rowing more during the day and less at night. I would take just an hour off now before returning for my last shift of the day. I set the alarm on my watch and lay down on my bunk, my hands behind my head, and smiled wryly as I thought about my sad and confused former self. From the perspective of the ocean it was so obvious to me that my goal—happiness—and the way that I was trying to achieve it—doing a job that eroded my self-confidence and my soul—had been utterly at odds with each other. I had clung for far too long to the illusion that material things were going to bring me joy, and this illusion had blinded me to the simple truth that happiness is a state of mind, and that while my life was dominated by unhappy thoughts not all the riches under the sun could make me a happy person. I remembered the day when things began to change, when the light began to break through my blindness.

It was a January morning, much like any other January morning in London—chilly and drizzly. The alarm went off at 6:15 A.M. Daybreak was still a couple of hours away. I immediately swung my feet out of bed and got up before I had a chance to think twice about it. We got ready to go to work, my husband and I moving through our usual workday routine, our movements between bedroom and bathroom and coffee pot perfected by the habit of years. We left the house on schedule, at 6:50, and crossed the bridge over the River Thames to the railway station, cars and trucks blasting us with exhaust fumes and spray from the wet road as they sped past. We stopped at the newsstand to buy our daily papers and then stood on the train platform in the darkness, waiting for the 7:11. I stared blankly at the derelict buildings on the opposite side of the tracks, feeling depressed.

I didn't want to go to work. I couldn't see the point of the project I was doing. I wasn't getting along with my boss. I hated that I arrived at the office in the darkness and left in darkness. It seemed like months since I had felt the sun on my skin. I wanted to go back home and curl up in bed and hibernate until the spring came.

But I didn't. I did what a responsible adult is supposed to do. I stood and I waited for the train. The 7:11 arrived and my husband and I got on. We sat down in our usual seats and opened our newspapers. But I was distracted. My eyes moved along the lines of print but I wasn't taking in the words. What was wrong with me today? A feeling of being disconnected from my life had been bubbling underneath the surface for some time now, and it seemed stronger today. I had a squirmy, squeamish feeling in my stomach. It felt similar to a guilty conscience, a physical discomfort, as if I were doing something wrong.

But that couldn't be. I was doing what I was supposed to do—working my way up the corporate ladder and the property ladder. Financial security and material comfort—this was what I had aspired to, ever since I had experienced the California lifestyle at the age of sixteen. Since then I had believed that this aspirational striving would ultimately lead to fulfilment and happiness. If I wasn't happy yet, it must surely be because I didn't yet have enough money or a big enough house. When I had those things, surely *then* I would be happy.

But somehow the logic of this now seemed faulty to me. Something was nagging at me, but I couldn't put my finger on it. What was the cause of my malaise?

My gaze wandered idly around the train car. It settled on the man sitting opposite me, reading a newspaper. He was of indeterminate age, probably about fifty but maybe not as old as he looked. He was wearing a suit with a navy raincoat over the top. His neck bulged over the tightness of his collar and tie. The skin of his face was saggy and gray. His nose was mottled purple with burst capillaries. His eyes behind his reading glasses were bloodshot and dull. He looked as if every ounce of youthful energy, every vestige of enthusiasm for life, every iota of idealism, had been sucked out of him. He seemed bored and world weary.

He felt my eyes staring at him and looked up. I glanced away long enough to break the embarrassing eye contact and then looked back at him. He had returned his attention to his newspaper and had turned the page. The side now facing me was the obituaries page. Obituaries—an entire person in all their complexity, summed up in a few paragraphs. The headlines of a life. What would people say about me when I died? Would I be worth an obituary? Or would I just pass away unnoticed, my life as fleeting and insignificant as a mayfly's? Would I end up like the man sitting opposite me, merely existing, rather than living?

Damn it! Wasn't I better than that? Didn't I deserve more out of this life than this grindingly dull routine and this pointless job?

Or did I? There was nothing special about me. I wasn't even very good at my job and even though I despised the job, this underachievement bothered me. If I couldn't do well at something that didn't matter, then what made me think I could do well at something that did? Apart from being a management consultant, what else was I qualified for?

In that tiny moment, the entire thread of thought lasting no more than a minute or two, a tiny fracture had appeared in my façade of normality. I had been living a conventional life, doing what I thought I was supposed to do, conforming to the norm, and following the crowd. Now that mask had cracked, and for a moment I had glimpsed What Might Be. Or indeed, *Who* Might Be. Could there really be a more interesting and independent person behind there, waiting to emerge into the light?

As the train rolled on toward Waterloo Station, my mind was starting to seethe with questions. I realized I had never truly gotten to know myself. I had been too willing to accept what other people told me about who I should be. Who was I really? And if I could be whoever I wanted, who would I be in the future? Did I have the courage to move forward and explore alternative possibilities?

I came up with a plan.

That night, I sat at my desk with two blank sheets of paper in front of me. I had decided to write my own obituary. What might people say about me when I died? Or, more importantly, how would I perceive my life as it was drawing to a close? Would I be proud of the way I'd lived, or full of regrets? I was going to write two versions. The first version would be the obituary that I wanted to have, and the second would be the one I was heading for if I carried on as I was.

Before I started on the first one, I thought of the obituaries that I had enjoyed reading, the people that I admired—they were people who dared to live life fearlessly, people who set out to experience the world and embrace life in all its variety. They might occasionally screw up spectacularly, fail gloriously, but they would pick themselves up and carry on trying. They wouldn't give a damn what anybody else thought of them—they lived life by their own rules, guided by their own principles. These were the adventurers and risk takers, the people who seemed to have lived many lifetimes in one. They dared to dream, and dream big. They set themselves goals and didn't allow self-doubt to sabotage their efforts. They made their lives matter. I scribbled down a description of my idealized self, not allowing myself to be constrained by any self-imposed limitations or by my present reality. In this obituary I had all the skills, all the character traits, all the internal resources I needed to live a glorious, successful, happy life. My pen flew across the paper, and I could feel a new zest for life bubbling up inside me. I felt energized and empowered, and excited about this life that could be mine, for even as I wrote I started to believe that this fantasy could come true. I finished writing and looked with satisfaction at the words on the page. In my imagination I had already lived this life, and was justly proud of my accomplishments. I felt not just happy, but joyful and inspired.

Then I came to the second obituary—the one that I was heading for. My pen moved more slowly this time, and I stopped frequently to chew the cap. My energy level subsided, and my enthusiasm slowly ebbed away. Even though this was my real life, and the first version had been an imaginary life, I'd had no difficulty covering a full page for my fantasy obituary while now I was struggling to find something interesting to write for the real one. After half a page of apathetic note writing I gave up. The second obituary described a conventional, ordinary life—pleasant, with a few moments of excitement—but leaving no legacy except a house clearance sale and a few friends with fond memories.

I looked at the two sheets of paper lying side by side on the table in front of me. The difference between the two, and the difference between how I had felt as I was writing them, was startling. I realized then that if I carried on living as I was, I would not end up with the life that I wanted. As I lay on my deathbed I wanted to be able to look back over my life and be proud of what I had achieved, but that wasn't where I was going—at the moment I was heading straight for mediocrity. Clearly something was going to have to change.

That day, I was a world away from being the person in my dream obituary. It had given me a clearer idea of where I wanted to go, but I had no idea how to get there. The longest journey begins with the first step, but I didn't have the courage to make even that first move, because I knew instinctively that once I set off down that path there would be no turning back, and I was afraid of where it might lead me. I had glimpsed a life of infinite potential but I didn't have the self-confidence and self-belief to take my dreams off the page and translate them into reality. I wasn't happy with my life the way it was, but at least it was what I knew. It wasn't perfect, but it was comfortable.

What really disturbed me was that it was clear from my obituary exercise that I had spent most of my life laboring under a fundamental misconception. I had believed that material things were going to make me happy, but nowhere in my dream obituary was there a mention of money, property, or possessions. It now appeared evident that these things were utterly irrelevant to my notion of a fulfilling life. What mattered was what I did, not what I owned. This revelation shook me to my very core. I had been a loyal follower of the cult of materialism since the trip to San Diego when I was sixteen, and the last eleven years—my entire adulthood—had been spent in the pursuit of material wealth. Now the illusion had been shattered, and I was suffering the equivalent of crisis of faith. If possessions couldn't make me happy, then what would?

It was a big question, and I didn't want to acknowledge the answer. The fantasy obituary had made me feel happy, but that was not the life I was living. To live that life I would have to make some enormous changes, and the prospect terrified me. While I had been writing my mind had opened a door to new possibilities, and I had been eager to explore beyond, but now I wanted to run back to reality and slam shut the door to the magical new world I had discovered. The implications were too much for me to handle. It was time to shut the lid on this Pandora's box of foolish fantasies. I put my pen down, and hid the two sheets of paper in the bottom of a desk drawer.

I still had a few minutes of rest time left before my next rowing shift started, but I decided to get up early and return to the oars. I wasn't ready to revisit that next chapter of my life just yet, so I left my bunk and returned to my rowing seat as if to do penance for the guilt that rushed back along with the memories.

six

ONE STROKE AT A TIME

*a*n alarm clock was ringing. I emerged reluctantly from a dream in which I had been slowly working my way along a sumptuous buffet table of all my favorite things, loading up a big plate full of food. I had been just about to dig in, the first forkful on its way from plate to mouth, when my sleep was interrupted. As consciousness dawned I registered the fact that my bed was rocking, that my hands were cramped and sore, and that it was pitch dark. I groaned. I wasn't about to have a delicious dinner—I was still on a wet, cold rowboat, bobbing around on the Atlantic, with my tenth tedious day of rowing and freeze-dried food ahead of me. I rotated my right shoulder in its socket. It grated. No improvement in the tendinitis.

Other aches and pains were developing as well. I had developed saltwater sores on my backside from spending many hours a day sitting on the salty wet cushion of my rowing seat. One of these sores had become infected and had blown up into a full-scale boil, complete with white head, right on the part of my right buttock where I would normally sit. At the start of each rowing shift I would wriggle and squirm, shifting my weight to try and find a position where the pressure on the boil was bearable.

My hands were also suffering the side effects of the long hours of rowing. The kangaroo-skin gloves were proving very effective in preventing the blisters from bursting open and becoming vulnerable to infection, but I was still getting bubbles of liquid building up under the calluses on my palms. The combination of pressure from the blisters and general tenderness of the skin made my hands throb. During the night the muscles in my fingers would stiffen up, contracting my hands into claws. From my conversations with previous ocean rowers I had expected these things, but there was a further affliction that I had not expected; my fingernails had started to part company with my fingers, the white tips of my nails extending day by day, getting closer to the quick. I wondered if my fingernails would fall off completely.

When I'd mentioned it in a dispatch, an ocean rower friend had texted me to say: "Ah yes, the memories are coming back to me now. Fingernails bleeding from the pressure." This had made me feel uncharacteristically furious. Why had nobody warned me about these things? I was spending a lot of time these days feeling angry, sometimes at myself, for having got myself into this predicament, and sometimes at my ocean rowing mentors, for not having told me just how hard it was going to be. This latter anger was, in fairness, entirely unjustified. I had been so certain that I was going to enjoy this that I had screened out any input that contradicted my sunny view of how it was going to be. But I was tired and sore and sometimes it made me feel better to blame somebody other than myself.

I reached up and pressed the button on my solar-powered watch to turn off the alarm. I felt I'd hardly slept—it had been more like a series of fitful dozes that left me more tired than ever. I'd now begun to trust my boat not to disintegrate in the force of the waves, and learned to sleep in the recovery position, braced between the lee cloths, so that I wouldn't roll from side to side, but it still felt like a long time since I'd had a decent night's sleep. The pain in my shoulder kept waking me up, as did the crashing of the waves, the creak of the rudder, and the constant fear that I might without warning be run down by a container ship.

I turned on the headlamp that hung from a cord over my bunk. I undid the strap of the wristwatch that hung from the same cord and looked at it.

Damn! Five-fifteen in the morning. How could that be? Despite my troubled slumber, somehow I'd slept through the first alarm and missed my midnight shift again. I was trying yet another variation of my shift pattern, convinced that if I could only find the "right" schedule, rowing twelve to sixteen hours a day would somehow become easier. But this one wasn't working, either. My body simply refused to submit to the tyranny of the alarm clock— this was the only way I could explain this selective deafness that allowed me to wake at the slightest noise, apart from the one noise that was supposed to wake me. It seemed that my body wanted its rest and would not be denied.

I sighed, my conscience prickling. I'd set myself the target of rowing for sixteen hours a day, but had only managed this a couple of times since the race began.

"How do you expect to keep up with the others if you don't put the hours in?" demanded Mr. Competitive. "Lazy cow," jeered Mr. Self-Critical.

"Shut up," I snapped. "I'd like to see you try and do this. It's harder than it looks, you know." But their words goaded me into action.

The night had been chilly, so I was already fully dressed in fleece trousers and a warm top. With difficulty, I extricated myself from the sleeping bag and shuffled my way down to the end of the cabin nearest the exit hatch. I turned on the cabin light and braced myself with my back against the food crate and my feet against the opposite wall to stop myself being pitched around with the motion of the boat. I folded back the thin mattress of my bunk to get to the hatch underneath, and pulled out a snack bar. Peeling back the cellophane wrapper I munched on the carob-topped nut and seed bar while I reached for my logbook. The 9Bar was a satisfying combination of sweetness, crunchiness, and gooeyness—almost as good as the fine foods of my dreamtime buffet. I turned on the chartplotter to find out if the wind and current had handed me a few bonus miles while I slept. The chartplotter blinked into life, showing a blue screen warning me that it was no substitute for paper charts. I knew this—that it was important to keep a note of my latitude and longitude at regular intervals, so that if all my navigation instruments failed I could still give my latest position to the rescue services if I needed them to come and get me. To conserve precious electricity I now turned down the brightness on the display to its dimmest setting, and hit the enter button to acknowledge the warning. A chart appeared on the screen, showing a large expanse of blue with a blinking dot in the middle. The dot represented my boat. Extending from the dot were two lines pointing to the left. One represented the shortest possible line between me and Antigua. The other was the direction I was currently drifting. Very occasionally the two lines coincided, but so far that had been rare. To date my progress across the ocean was a wiggly line meandering erratically west-southwest.

A set of numbers across the top of the screen gave me the information I needed for my logbook entry. I took up my pencil, my stiff fingers struggling to grip it firmly, and opened the logbook to the latest page of neatly ruled columns. I jotted down the latitude and longitude of my present position, and the distance and bearing to Antigua.

I sighed: 329 miles down, 2607 to go. The scale of the task ahead seemed overwhelming. And sleeping through my night shifts wasn't helping me get there any sooner.

I also wrote down the wind speed and direction, as well as the level of charge in my two solar-powered batteries, and gave myself marks out of five for physical and mental well-being. Two out of five for physical—my shoulders were aching badly and I was relying heavily on painkillers from my extensive first-aid kit—and two out of five for mental. My pre-race optimism had long since evaporated. The rest of the race fleet was pulling away, and although I was still in contention with a few tail enders I was going more slowly than I'd hoped. The lack of progress was getting me down. My one corporate cash sponsor had offered to double its modest contribution if I beat the current women's record of fifty-six days for the crossing. I had been excited by the prospect, and it had helped keep me going through the long hours of training, but now my mental and physical resources were at a low ebb, and even the offer of hard cash failed to motivate me.

It was time to check in with my mother. When I had first told her about my plans, fourteen months previously, I had been surprised by her lack of reaction to the news. "Mum, I'm going to row alone across the Atlantic Ocean." You might have thought that it would generate *some* kind of a response, favorable or otherwise. But no, there was just a "Hmmm," and she changed the subject. I was left feeling that I had committed some kind of faux pas in even mentioning it—as if I had inadvertently blurted out some heinous swearword and she was tactfully choosing to ignore my outburst. It was only later that she confessed that she hoped that if she ignored it, the whole horrible idea might go away. But time went by and it became clear that it was not going to disappear—on the contrary, with every passing day I was becoming more deeply committed to my crazy scheme. To Mum's eternal credit, she then decided to take the attitude "if you can't beat 'em, join 'em," and had become one of my staunchest supporters, even coming to live on the south coast of England with me for a month to help with final preparations for the race. She had worked on the boat, packaged up rations, assembled my first-aid kit, made little bags and pockets on her sewing machine, and helped me make the cabin as comfortable and homey as it could be. In short, she had done her best to make sure her daughter would be warm, safe, and well fed. Without her help I would have struggled to do all that needed to be done in that hectic final month, and I'd like to think that her participation helped her as well, for she got to know my boat as well as I did, and she knew that *Sedna* was well equipped and seaworthy.

That month had been a special time, bringing me and my mother closer than we had been since I was in my early teens. In many ways she was still playing the role of mother, cooking meals for me and making items on her sewing machine—although now the sewing machine was electric and she was sewing cockpit bags rather than cute little-girl dresses—but in other ways, for the first time, we were relating to each other as adults rather than mother and child. She was involved in almost every aspect of my preparations, and our shared focus bonded us closely. Experiencing this intense time together created shared memories, shared stories, and shared jokes—in-jokes that would have us both giggling like teenagers, to the mystification of bystanders. Although I may not have told her so at the time, and she would probably have been embarrassed if I had, I found her company a real delight, as well as helpful beyond measure.

I hadn't originally intended that she would become my shore manager as well as my housekeeper and boatfitter. In the big-budget world of professional yacht racing, solo sailors might have a support team of up to thirty-five people helping to organize every aspect of their campaign. This team could include meteorologists, technicians, electricians, webmasters, public relations agents, sponsorship organizers, personal trainers, nutritionists, physiologists, and psychologists.

Me? I had my mother. And my mother was, for all her many strengths and virtues, and with no disrespect intended, none of the above. But she came free of charge, and my options had been limited.

There had been a couple of very suitable contenders, but both had dropped out, reinforcing my opinion that the only person I could truly rely on was myself—and my mother. She knew nothing about the ocean nor the weather, but she did know a lot about me. There was no need for me to keep up appearances with her. I was finding that I could tell her exactly how I was feeling and know that it would stay between us. It was good to be able to talk to someone who would give me her wholehearted support no matter what happened, and whom I could trust not to tell anybody else about my doubts and struggles. Without her sympathy and understanding, I reflected, the burden of my self-imposed predicament would be almost too much to bear. Sometimes I pictured her standing in front of me like a lioness defending her cubs, trying to fight back the voices of Mr. Self-Doubt, Mr. Self-Critical, and Mr. Competitive.

I took the Iridium satellite phone out of its waterproof case and connected it to the cable that led out through the roof of my cabin to an external aerial. I turned it on and it scanned the skies for a satellite signal. After a minute or so it stopped scanning and displayed the word *Iridium* to let me know it was ready. The phone beeped to signal the arrival of a text message—the daily Woodvale weather forecast. I scanned the words, trying to make sense of them. After my pre-race correspondence course in meteorology and navigation I knew a little more about weather and forecasts than my mother did, but not much.

LOW PRESSURE 934MB 032.32W 27.56N DEEPENING MOVING WNW. NW WINDS 20 TO 25 KT WITH GUSTS TO 35 KT . . .

INCREASING TO 25 TO 30 KT WITH GUSTS TO AROUND 40 KT
LATE. SEAS 8 TO 10 FT. SHOWERS LIKELY.

I understood "Showers likely," but little else. The winds
sounded alarming, but I couldn't be sure whether they would actually affect me. This same forecast was sent to all the rowing boats
in this very large swath of the ocean, so the conditions it described
might be hundreds of miles away. If I'd had the energy to get out
my Atlantic charts, plot the location of the low pressure, and work
out my position in relation to it I might have had a better idea of
what was headed my way, but it all seemed more trouble than it
was worth. The charts were huge, my cabin was small, it wasn't easy
to plot a position on a violently lurching boat while sitting cross-
legged. Quite frankly, I couldn't be bothered. There was nothing I
could do about it anyway. Unlike a sailing boat, I wasn't moving
fast enough to take advantage of favorable winds or avoid adverse
ones. I just had to cope with whatever weather the ocean chose to
dole out to me, taking the rough with the smooth.

I deleted the weather forecast and dialed my mother's number.
I started to mentally compile a list of things I wanted to mention.
Calls from my satellite phone cost $1.50 a minute so we tried to
keep our conversations short and businesslike. This was easy to do,
as my mother's focus is always on the practical. If I started off on a
self-indulgent litany of complaints she would swiftly pull me back
to what needed to be done to address them, forcing me to think in
terms of action rather than emotion.

"Hello?" I heard the reassuring sound of my mother's voice.

"Hi, Mum, it's me."

"Hello, Rosalind," she said with a warmth that told me how
relieved she was to hear that I was still alive. She is the only person
in the world who still calls me by my full name, and although I
don't especially like my full name, I wouldn't have it any other way.

We talked for about ten minutes. She brought me up to date with what was happening elsewhere in the racing fleet. The crews were already scattered across a broad area. I was a long way behind the men's fours, but I wasn't in last position, which gave me hope. There were a number of pairs behind me, and I kept trading positions with Chris Martin, the solo male competitor.

"How is *Charmed Life* doing?" I asked.

"They're gaining on you. It looks like they'll overtake you in the next few days."

In one of the more bizarre stories of the 2005 Atlantic Rowing Race, a crew—originally called *One Life*—had suffered catastrophe within the first few days of the race when one of the two crew members, Andrew Morris, fell over on deck and cracked his head. He ended up in the hospital with a concussion and it looked as if his race was over, especially when his French crewmate returned home to Paris. Not to be deterred, Andrew managed to press-gang a substitute. Mick Dawson was a Woodvale employee and a veteran of one Atlantic crossing and two failed Pacific attempts. He had been an invaluable help to me as I prepared for my race. With the safety consciousness born of twice ending up in a life raft on the Pacific, he had advised me well on how to make my boat as safe as possible. Now Andrew would also benefit from Mick's ocean-rowing experience. This hastily assembled crew, renamed *Charmed Life,* set off six days after the rest of the field so now it was rather depressing to have them breathing down my neck when I'd had such a substantial head start. They were two big strong guys, it's true, and I was just, well, I was just me—but nevertheless it irked me to be overtaken. I had the worst of both worlds: I was competitive enough to hate being beaten, but not competitive enough to force myself to row more hours in the day to improve my race position. If I could have powered my boat with the force of my yearning to be back on dry land, I'd have been speeding along at five knots. But ocean rowboats do not respond to psychological power, only raw muscle, and so I trundled along at my sedate two knots, knowing that wishing alone would not get me there any faster.

"Has the money come through from the sponsor yet?" I asked.

"No. I checked your account this morning, and still nothing. You're close to your overdraft limit. It's just as well you're not actually spending anything while you're out on the ocean apart from your Iridium bill."

Despite my strenuous efforts, it looked as if my sponsorship drive had largely failed. Numerous leads, initially promising, had come to nothing. Then, just one week before I'd left to travel to the Canaries, I had been promised £25,000 ($50,000 U.S.) by an American businessman as a result of an informal introduction. But that had been more than six weeks ago now and still the money had not materialized.

"Have you emailed him?"

"Yes, and he says he's still working on getting the money together. He hopes to get it to you by the end of the week."

The sponsorship saga would drag on for a few more weeks, with repeated promises and repeated disappointment. The money never did arrive—further reinforcing my reluctant conclusion that I should rely on nobody but myself.

"How are you feeling today?" she asked once we had covered business matters.

"Well, OK, I suppose. Still finding it tough. But they said the first two weeks would be the hardest part, so I hope things are going to start getting easier soon. This isn't much fun so far."

"Oh, Rosalind." Her voice conveyed her concern. She could have reminded me that I'd chosen to do this, or told me to pull myself together, or pointed out that she hadn't wanted me to do this in the first place. But she refrained from all these tempting responses. She said exactly the right thing.

"Here's a big hug. And there'll be an even bigger hug waiting for you when you get to Antigua."

"Thanks, Mum. Big hug to you, too. I'll call you tomorrow. Bye."

I pressed the red button to end the phone call, disconnected the aerial, and put the handset away in its case. I looked at my watch and sighed: 5:45. I didn't feel much like rowing, but this boat wasn't going to row itself to Antigua. Time to get on with it.

I finished my nut and seed bar and got ready to start rowing. I took off my fleece pants and put on yesterday's T-shirt and a long-sleeved top—and that was all. No matter how chilly it was outside, I found life much easier if I wore nothing on my bottom half. I was far from convinced by the theory that rowing naked prevented saltwater sores (my backside provided ample evidence to the contrary) but the fewer clothes I wore the better, because any garments would only get soaked in seawater and would then lie around in damp little piles going moldy.

I reached into the wall pockets for a pack of painkillers. On dry land I'd rarely even take an aspirin, but these were special circumstances. The previous day I had made a mistake. I had taken a Co-Proxamol tablet but it had no effect, so I stepped up to a Tramadol—and then remembered too late that Woodvale had warned us that they are potent pain relievers but can knock you flat. I had started feeling very light-headed, sleepy, and uncoordinated. I tried taking some chocolate as an antidote, hoping the sugar and caffeine might help bring me to my senses, but the experiment was not a success. I had felt as spaced out as ever. I wouldn't have minded the side effects so much if there had been any benefits from the drug, but my shoulder was as excruciatingly painful as before.

It had been alarming to find myself feeling so out of control. On a rocking boat like this it would only take one careless moment, one stumble, and I could find myself literally in very deep water, with nobody around to throw me a lifeline. Before the race one of my greatest fears had been that I would do something trivial that on dry land would have no great consequences, but on the ocean could prove to be my undoing. For this reason, I had done all I could in advance to idiot-proof my boat. As well as the grab lines along her sides in case I fell in the water, I had placed grab handles in strategic positions around the cockpit, and my spare oars served as guardrails, giving me plenty of things to hang on to as I moved around the boat.

A product sponsor had given me a specially adapted safety harness with a bungee cord attached to a D-ring on the back, rather than the front, so that it wouldn't get in the way while I was rowing. I had promised my mother that I would wear it all the time, but I had found it too inhibiting, so after the first few days it was consigned to a storage hatch and only reemerged on very few occasions when conditions were especially hostile.

So far my fears of life-terminating clumsiness seemed unfounded. I was finding that my instinct for self-preservation seemed sharper on the ocean, and I was quietly pleased with my apparent ability to look after myself. (So take *that*, Mr. Self-Critical—I'm not as clumsy as you think I am.) I was keenly aware that I needed to take good care of myself and of my body. I knew that a number of ocean rows had ended prematurely due to injury—hatches slamming onto heads, rowers falling and injuring their backs, people being flung across their cabin by a rogue wave.

To avoid this last hazard I had considered various options: one ocean rower had worn a crash helmet while he slept, but this sounded too uncomfortable. Other people had strapped them-selves to their bunk to avoid being tossed around, but I didn't like the possibility of ending up tethered to a sinking ship. So I had taken the advice of a rower who had installed lee cloths on either side of his bunk—canvas strips about six feet long and eighteen inches wide, anchored by a batten along their lower edge, with the top edge suspended from pulleys on the ceiling of the cabin. I would have reason to be grateful for the lee cloths on more than one occasion, when a wave tipped the boat and I found myself bouncing off yielding cloth rather than solid cabin wall.

I rubbed Deep Heat cream into my aching shoulders, struggling to contort myself sufficiently to get it where it needed to go—right between my shoulder blades, on either side of my spine. Then I put on a warm hat and a headlamp, sighed again, and opened the hatch to the cockpit. It was still dark, and the cold wind hit me with a bracing slap. I went out headfirst through the round hatch and stood for a moment on the deck, holding on to the stainless-steel grab bar behind me and looking out across the black, choppy ocean, flecked here and there with white foaming wave crests. It seemed like a long time since I had seen dry land. This was my world now, a world of sea and sky and clouds. And though each day the scenery was infinitely different—a sunrise could be red or pink or yellow or gray, the ocean could be green or blue or black or silver—at the same time it was depressingly monotonous. No mountains, no trees, no towns or villages—just day after day of ocean. One of the reasons I had wanted to cross the Atlantic on my own was so I could get a better sense of the scale of the planet, but the scheme had worked almost too well. I did indeed have a sense of the scale of the planet and of the ocean—and it was very, very big. There were times when I felt as if I were rowing the same piece of ocean over and over again, like a runner on a treadmill. The weather changed, but the scenery never varied from sky above, water below.

On this particular morning there was no moon, and only the faint glow of starlight lit the cockpit. I turned on my headlamp, put on my shoes, and stepped over to my rowing seat. I badly missed the sensation of walking. I liked to walk—it always seemed to clear my head and stimulate my brain—but since the race started I hadn't taken more than two consecutive steps. And even the two steps from the hatch to the rowing position were taken at a stoop as I moved from handhold to handhold, always hanging on as my boat tipped unpredictably from side to side. My back was constantly rounded—while rowing, while walking the two steps, while sitting in my cabin. At the end of each shift I would go back to my standing position in front of the cabin hatch, hang on to the grab bar, and arch my lower back to try and straighten it out, but it wasn't enough to counteract the aching stiffness.

I gingerly lowered my naked buttocks onto the cushion of the rowing seat. This was my least favorite moment of the day. My skin was still warm from my sleeping bag and the cold, clammy cushion felt deeply unpleasant. I shuddered involuntarily. Dawdling over my preparations to put off the moment when I would have to start rowing again, I carefully pulled on my kangaroo-skin gloves and tightened the Velcro straps across the backs of my hands. I released the handles of the stowed oars from their hooked brackets on the side decks (platforms about six inches wide running the length of the cockpit along the sides of the boat), then released the rudder strings from the toothed cleats that had held the rudder in place overnight. I turned on the red light in the compass between my feet—red so it wouldn't disrupt my night vision—and took a look at the bearing. The boat had turned beam to the waves while I slept, and I needed to turn her through ninety degrees to point myself in the right direction for Antigua. I tilted my foot to adjust the rudder and started rowing, left arm only, to turn the boat. The wind was blowing strongly enough to make it hard work to pull the boat around until it was perpendicular to the wind and the waves. I counted the one-handed strokes until I was pointing the right way. Forty-eight, forty-nine, fifty. I checked the compass again. That would do it. I took a deep breath and took my first full stroke of the day. One stroke down. By the end of today I would have rowed another ten thousand.

Ten thousand strokes. Oh boy. Two, three, four, five ...

The weather had been overcast and cold for the last few days, so my solar-powered batteries were running low and I couldn't afford to waste electricity on running the stereo. I had planned to use music to help me through the day, but so far it was proving unfeasible. The absence of musical entertainment, especially in the dark when there was no visual stimulation, either, made for rather tedious rowing. I focused on counting the strokes.

Twelve, thirteen, fourteen, fifteen ...

I was sitting right on my boil. I wriggled on the seat, trying to rest my weight somewhere else.

Twenty, twenty-one, twenty-two ...

My shoulders creaked complainingly. The painkillers hadn't kicked in yet, and the grating pain dominated my thoughts.

Twenty-nine, thirty, thirty-one ...

Less than two minutes into the shift, and I was bored already. Yet this had seemed like such a good idea at the time.

It had been summer 2004, and I barely recognized myself as the same person who had once yearned for the approval of corporate bosses or ransomed her happiness to material possessions. I had first dipped my toe into the world of adventure with an extended trip to Peru in 2003. I had spent three months there on my own, exploring, trekking, and mountaineering. This first foray had gone well and boosted my confidence in my ability to survive—and indeed thrive—alone, trusting my instincts and allowing the universe to look after me.

That spring, inspired by Henry David Thoreau's *Walden*, I had spent a month alone in a remote cottage on the west coast of Ireland. It had been an intensely formative time. I'd gone there with a rucksack full of books on science, philosophy, and religion, chosen fairly randomly—some I had purchased, others were from a friend's library of books. Strangely, a common message had emerged from this eclectic selection: that the way humans are treating the planet, polluting it and exploiting its resources, is unsustainable. Unless we start to take better care of the planet, our days here will be numbered. Even before my self-imposed retreat in Ireland I had already started to develop a personal code of beliefs and behaviors to guide me in my new life, and in that rich new soil these seeds of wisdom had found fertile ground.

Now, in the summer of 2004, I had no job, no home, no money, and I was separated from my husband. This may sound deeply traumatic, but in fact life was spontaneous, exciting, and fun. For the first time in my life I had no particular purpose or long-term plan, and the seeds that had been sown in Ireland were able to come to fruition. I was living rent-free in a tiny eighteenth-century flat above an antiques shop in Richmond, southwest London, after the shopkeeper had taken pity on me when I went into his shop to try and sell an old watch to raise some cash. I was maintaining a trickle of income from selling off my possessions and baking organic cakes for a farmers' market. I had just enough money, and plenty enough time, to pursue my newfound curiosity. For the previous fifteen years I had been bound by obligations and duty, but now I had managed to extricate myself from most of the shackles of conventional adulthood, and for the first time in my life I felt free. But something was missing—I needed a sense of purpose.

I'd had a number of ideas, but none of them had seemed quite right. All my life I had suffered from the dual curse of enthusiasm and impatience. The enthusiasm that burned twice as bright often burned only half as long. I'd had a significant number of passing projects, many of which had been abandoned before coming to fruition, usually overtaken by a new passion. Handicrafts projects were relegated to a cupboard or passed off to my mother for completion. Languages were studied avidly but interest flagged once I progressed to the subtleties of subordinate clauses and subjunctives. Business plans were devised and documented but never put into action. Recently I had toyed with various schemes, but in each case I hesitated before the scheme made it off the drawing board and into reality. Sometimes I decided that the planning had been enough of an education in itself, or doubts set in about the worth of the project.

I will never know how my life might have turned out if I had taken one of those alternative paths. Maybe the ideas were fundamentally flawed, or maybe the will to make them happen just faded away. It is possible there is no such a thing as a bad idea—only ideas that lack the commitment to see them through to fruition. But my lack of what my mother called "stickability" was starting to concern me. I feared I was starting to look like a dreamer rather than a doer. It was time to find a project that fired my enthusiasm and was in tune with my personal values, a project that I could commit to and see through to its natural conclusion.

I remember the precise moment I decided to row the Atlantic. I was driving along the highway in my camper van on a sunny English summer day. I wasn't thinking about anything in particular. Various thoughts were just wandering around aimlessly inside my head, unguided by any conscious direction. The thoughts, roughly speaking, were these:

I had recently received the first installment of my divorce settlement and it was burning a hole in my pocket. It wasn't enough to buy a home of bricks and mortar, so I'd been looking at live-aboard boats as a viable alternative. I had never spent much time around boats or boating people before, but as I'd got to know the boating community I'd been impressed with their sense of community and comradeship, bonded by a love of an unconventional and itinerant lifestyle. Boats had come to be associated in my mind with a spirit of adventure.

My studies in Ireland were still fresh in my mind. I wanted to see more of this planet before we degraded it even further. But I did not want my travels to hasten those changes, so whatever means of transport I chose would have to be environmentally friendly.

I'd raced in a couple of marathons over the previous few years, drawn to the event by people telling me that I would find out things about myself in the last few miles of a marathon. This had been my motivation—the possibility of greater self-knowledge—but the marathon failed to enlighten. Maybe 26.2 miles just wasn't far enough, and I needed a longer physical challenge, or even an adventure, but I didn't seem qualified to do much. I didn't know how to climb, sail, or survive in arctic conditions.

I was increasingly enjoying my own company, and the sense of self-reliance it engendered. I was growing as a person, discovering abilities and strengths that I hadn't known I possessed, and I suspected there were more. But being rather lazy by nature I knew I had to put myself in a situation where I would have to fend for myself and not depend on someone else for assistance. I also wanted to find out who I was when I was alone—when I was not reacting to the expectations of others. Who was I when I was not being someone's wife, girlfriend, daughter, sister, colleague, friend? So my new project had to be solo.

Most importantly, I wanted to make a contribution to the greater good. It may have been partly due to the influence of my parents, who spent their lives in dutiful service to others, but I felt a strong need to leave a legacy. I knew I was unlikely to have children, so I wanted to find some other way to make my mark. I needed to believe that my time on this earth would leave the world a slightly better place than it had been when I arrived. During my years in the office I knew that this was not the way—not for me, at least. I needed to find a project that would enable me to touch people's lives in a positive way—heart to heart, not wallet to wallet.

And recently I had read a book by Debra Veal, who had set out with her husband, Andrew, to compete in the Atlantic Rowing Race of 2001. She was petite and blond, while he was six-foot-five and 240 pounds. But despite his strapping build, within the first few days of the row it had become apparent that Andrew was not coping psychologically with the challenge. Claustrophobia inside the tiny cabin and a fear of the ocean conspired to incapacitate him totally. He was lifted from the boat by the support yacht. Debra, however, was relishing her time on the ocean, and decided to carry on alone. She arrived in Barbados, 116 days later, to a media frenzy. She had shown that ocean rowing is more about strength of mind than strength of muscle, and that perseverance mattered more than size. It had been an inspiring story, like many of the other inspiring adventure books I had read, but rowing across the Atlantic had not struck me then as something that I would want to do. Now, however . . .

These were the notions knocking around in my head: boats, adventure, environmental awareness, endurance, solitude, contribution, rowing . . .

Flash! I know! I'll row the Atlantic! I nearly veered off the highway when the thought hit me with all the force of a thunderbolt.

My first thought was "This is so perfect. This is the best idea I've ever had."

My second thought was "This is the worst idea I ever had. I can't possibly do this. It's insane—too big, too scary."

I spent the rest of the journey, and the rest of the week, trying to talk myself out of it, but the idea refused to go away. I woke up every morning thinking of more reasons why rowing an ocean was the ideal project for me. I had never before been so convinced that something was right. This idea may have seemed crazy, but it had struck me with such force that I just had to see if I could make it work. It had seemed to come from outside of myself, as if for a moment my ego had been put to one side—my ego with all its self-serving fears and self-imposed limitations, my ego that did not dare to dream big for fear of failing big. In that one life-changing moment, I had tapped into a deeper consciousness that had produced this almost divine flash of inspiration.

Despite my best efforts to argue it out of existence, by the end of that week I had reached the stage where I simply had to do it, or spend the rest of my life wondering, "if only."

It would be a huge challenge, but I believed I could do it. It seemed to strike just the right balance between challenging yet doable. It was an ambitious plan, undoubtedly, but it felt as if everything in my life so far had been leading me to this point. I knew exactly *what* I wanted to do, and *why* I wanted to do it. I'd just have to figure out the *how* as I went along.

In my mind, I was committed. It was perfect.

seven

ONE OAR DOWN

*M*y eleventh day at sea was a Saturday, and it brought a Saturday night to remember. I was experimenting with yet another pattern of rowing shifts, still hoping that there was a schedule that would make the days and miles pass more quickly. I had decided to ditch the night shifts again, and revert to a plan where I would take shorter breaks during the day so that I could take a longer rest at night. I hoped that this would give my body a better chance to recover.

It was one o'clock in the morning when I finished my last shift. It had been a long day, and the final hour had been a battle of wills between my weary body and my stubborn mind. My body wanted to quit early, so I'd had to coax it along, telling it "just a hundred more strokes," and then another hundred, and another. When it truly was the last one hundred strokes, I promised it an uninterrupted six hours of rest, and with this reward in prospect, we made it through to the end of the day.

As I stowed the oars for the night I glanced at the red ensign, flapping in the darkness from its pole on the roof of my sleeping cabin. Uh-oh. It was flapping in the wrong direction, back toward the roof rather than forward toward me, which meant that the wind had shifted around and was blowing from the south. This was bad news, as south was where I wanted to go. In that direction lay the so-called conveyor belt of trade winds that would, I hoped, whisk me toward Antigua. So far the winds had generally been blowing me in the right direction—anything west or south was fine with me—but this tricky little wind was now threatening to blow me north. Even if I rowed all night I would probably still be blown off course, because ocean rowboats are not designed to row upwind, their bulky cabins creating too much wind resistance to allow forward progress. It looked like I would have to deploy the sea anchor to try to mitigate my northward drift.

I opened up the hatch to the fore cabin of my boat and pulled out the lumpy bag that held the sea anchor. I had bought it sec-ondhand from another ocean rower. It looked rather scruffy and faded, its green and yellow fabric stained with rust marks, but buying a used one had saved me a substantial sum of money. The anchor consisted of a fabric parachute on a rope one hundred yards long. When deployed it held about a ton of seawater, suspended just below the waves, which acted like a brake to stop the boat being blown backward. It could also be used to stabilize the boat in rough conditions by holding the craft perpendicular to the pre-vailing wind so that the waves would glance along the boat's sides rather than attacking it beam on.

Before the race started, James "Tiny" Little, the British rower who had sold me the anchor, had come out with me in *Sedna* one day to show me how to deploy it. I had been delighted to see Tiny arrive in La Gomera to see us off for the start of the race. Tiny was a pub landlord from Norwich. He had appeared quietly on the pontoon next to my boat, clad in shorts and a polo shirt. "Hello, Roz," he said, in his low-key, deadpan drawl, as if I'd just walked into his pub to order a drink, rather than being about to set out on the biggest adventure of my life. "Tiny!" It was good to see his familiar cheery face, his eyes twinkling above a shy smile. Tiny was an unlikely endurance athlete. Over the years his health had fallen victim to his occupation—he had been overweight and out of shape, before deciding to turn himself around. He had lost weight, got fit, and rowed the Atlantic in slow but magnificent style earlier that same year. He had celebrated passing significant milestones with beer chilled in his onboard mini refrigerator and had posted hugely entertaining updates to his website. During my preparations he had been generous with words of sensible advice, and now he came to the dock bearing gifts—a spare power inverter that I had asked him to get for me, five bars of Ritters chocolate (rum, raisin, and hazelnut flavor, now slightly melting in the Canarian sunshine), and a homemade Christmas pudding. When he offered to show me how to use the sea anchor, I was quick to accept. I had scant seafaring experience, and there was much I needed to learn. Many ocean rowers had blithely talked about "drogues, sea anchors, and rodes." At the time I had not asked them to elaborate, since I was more focused on fitting out the boat than on skippering it, but as the race approached I grew concerned about my lack of seamanship. Tiny quite accurately assumed that we were starting from a low knowledge base and, without being patronizing, talked me through the process one step at a time. Now I screwed up my eyes in concentration, trying to remember exactly what he had told me to do. I cast my mind back to that sunny day in La Gomera, only a couple of weeks ago yet seemingly a different lifetime. We had paddled out of the harbor and a short distance along the coast, where we stopped in the lee of the island while he gave me my lesson in sea anchor management.

"This line here is your main line," he had said, holding a thick black rope that led from the towing eye on my bow back into the cockpit. "You need to attach this to the strings at the bottom of the chute with this shackle. Then you take this tripline"—he lifted a thinner, multicolored rope—"and attach it to the top of the chute. And you clip the other end to your boat so you don't lose it. We'll use this D-ring here." And he snapped the carabiner onto a convenient D-shaped bolt on *Sedna's* bulkhead. "Then you attach this buoy to the top of the chute as well, so it keeps the anchor at the right depth under the water. You want the anchor to be submerged under the waves but lying out in front of the boat, not beneath it."

He had gathered up the bulky armful of the chute and lifted it onto the side of the boat. "Now you deploy it. Make sure you put it out to the upwind side of the boat, so that as you get blown downwind, the anchor fills up with water and the rope gradually pays out over the side." He placed the anchor in the water, and it gently inflated until it looked like a huge green and yellow jellyfish, with its strings for tentacles. The black rope slowly ran out over *Sedna's* side as we got farther and farther from the anchor, until all we could see of it was the little white buoy that marked its position.

"Okay," Tiny said. "Now, when you want to pull it back in, you take this tripline"—he picked up the multicolored line again—"and you pull on it. Coil it into this bucket as you draw it in so it doesn't get tangled. And look how easy that is. It's collapsed the chute so you hardly need to put any effort in. Here it comes."

I looked over the side, and watched as he drew the chute back alongside the boat. I reached over and hoisted the dripping fabric on board, then coiled the black main line. We unclipped the tripline and put it away safely. I had just learned how to use one of the most important devices in the ocean rower's armory.

It had all seemed very easy in La Gomera that day with Tiny, with the sun shining and the sea relatively calm. Now it was dark and the wind was starting to blow gustily. By the light of my head-lamp I followed the steps that Tiny had showed me and soon Sid the sea anchor (as I had named him) had slid over the side into the darkened waters and was out on the end of his rope. Satisfied that all was set for the night, I retired to my cabin.

At half past three I was woken by violent rocking and the sound of waves crashing over my cabin roof. I stuck my head out the hatch and was greeted by a blast of wind and a scene of devastation. The wind had strengthened significantly in the last couple of hours and was wreaking havoc on the deck of my boat. Back in the cabin I hastily pulled on a waterproof jacket as token protection against the elements and launched myself out through the hatch, slamming it shut behind me before a wave could intrude. I quickly clipped on my safety harness and scrabbled around on all fours to retrieve various objects that were making a bid for freedom. I had secured most items on deck with cords and lashings, but even so, a few things were in danger of being lost to the waves. I managed to haul in a jerry can that was dangling by a bungee cord over the side of the boat, and rescued two buckets and a pair of running shoes that were floating around in the flooded footwell. The only escapee was a supersize pot of baby wipes—which I used as toilet paper—which was swept away by the waves and was last seen heading for Greenland. I paused briefly to glance at the navigation instruments and note the wind speed—twenty-two knots at that moment, but I found out later that the Woodvale race website said it had been gusting to sixty. The conditions were horribly hostile—fearsome waves were lashing the deck and the waters around me were as dark and glistening as coal—but I was too focused on trying to salvage vital equipment to have time to be scared. It would only be later that I would have time to reflect on what might have happened if I had suffered the same fate as the baby wipes.

With everything stowed I retreated for the night while the wind continued to blow. At one point the whole boat tipped onto its side and I found myself lying on a lee cloth instead of my mattress, until the boat slowly self-righted and I flopped back down onto my bunk. I was groggy with sleep when it happened, and although I was grumpy about my rude awakening, once again I didn't have time to be scared before it was all over—and by then there was no point in being scared because the situation had already passed and I was still in one piece. I was fine, but the knockdown took a toll on the shipshapeness of my boat. In the morning all sorts of things that normally lived on the right hand side of the cabin were found in unlikely lodging places on the left, and it took me more than an hour to restore order.

The next day the wind gradually eased but continued to come from the wrong direction, so Sid the sea anchor stayed out on his rope and the oars lay idle. After nearly two weeks of daily rowing it felt strange to be doing so little. Even though the wind was clearly against me and it would have been futile to row, I couldn't help feeling guilty. Mr. Guilt now joined Mr. Self-Doubt, Mr. Self-Critical, and Mr. Competitive as a regular visitor. I had set out with the intention of rowing sixteen hours a day and felt guilty that so far I had averaged only twelve—or today, none at all. If I'd had a crewmate to alternate their shifts with mine, I might have found it easier to congratulate myself at the end of each completed shift and enjoy some well-deserved rest. Instead my rest hours were tainted by the feeling that I was shirking my rowing duties and should be doing more. "You should be rowing, you should be rowing," chanted the insistent voices in my head.

To reassure myself that I was not being lazy I called Tiny from my satphone to make sure I was justified in not rowing. He told me what I needed to hear—that there was no point in rowing and I should make the most of the enforced idleness to allow my shoulders to recover. I relaxed slightly, and Mr. Guilt gave me a break.

That evening the weather was filthy—big waves, gusting winds, and pouring rain—and I was gobbling down a hastily prepared meal of freeze-dried cod and potato casserole, hunched over my food mug to protect it from being swamped by the waves that swept with annoying regularity over the gunwales. I could have eaten inside the cabin, but the boat was pitching around and I did not want to risk spilling food over my bunk, which would have made the cabin even more musty than it was already. I had thought I had emerged relatively unscathed (baby wipes notwithstanding) from the big blow of the previous night, but I was wrong. As I huddled in a corner of the deck, I glanced around and noticed that one of my oars was broken. Not broken in two—that I would have noticed immediately—but splintered along its length in four distinct cracks, like a plastic drinking straw that had been trodden on. This was not a major problem—yet. I had two spare oars, as well as a spare rowing seat and spare oarlocks—but I was surprised and concerned that the oar seemed to have broken so easily. I couldn't afford to lose my rowing equipment. I blamed myself for having stowed it too close to the water. The problem was that the cockpit of my boat, designed for a single rower, was not long enough for me to store the oars down on the deck as the pairs' boats could. I had been storing my spare oars in the "guardrail" position, so that the shaft of the oar served as a barrier along the side of the cockpit, but there was no easy place for my main set of oars to be stowed clear of the oarlocks. When I wasn't rowing, I had been leaving them in the oarlocks and hooking the handle under a hooked bar designed specially for the purpose, so that the oars lay flat along the gunwale at the side of the boat. But this gunwale was only about a foot above the water level, and as I had just discovered to my cost, the oars should have been stowed well clear of the treacherous waves.

"Well, that was stupid," said Mr. Self-Critical. "You could have seen that one coming."

"OK, OK," I growled. "So now I know. From now on the oars get stowed high up against the rollbar." I looked up at the bar that arced over the roof of my aft cabin. It had a bolted gate on each side for stowing my spare oars, but nowhere specifically designed for the other pair. Never mind, I could bungee them in place against the spares. That would put them about four feet above the water, and, I hoped, out of harm's way. In the meantime, I needed to swap out the broken oar and substitute a spare. After I'd finished my dinner I carefully undid the bolt on the hoop of stainless steel that held the spare oars in place, and took out the spare oar, replacing it with the broken one, which would now serve as a guardrail. I didn't want it to give way if I fell against it, so I looked around for something to use as a splint. Aha—I had just the thing.

I opened the hatch to the forward storage cabin and crawled in headfirst to get it. For no apparent reason I had decided when packing my boat that a long-handled boathook might be useful in the mid-Atlantic, and now its moment had come. My boat-builder, Richard Uttley, had thrown it in the trash can at least three times. "What do you want with a boathook in the middle of the ocean?" he had scoffed. "They're for hooking mooring buoys. You're not going to find any of those out there." But three times I had retrieved it and put it back on my boat. I was determined to have it on board, and now I knew why. I made a mental note to tell Richard that my intuition had been right.

I split the telescopic pole into its two sections and lashed one of them tightly to the broken oar with duct tape, wrapping the thick black tape around the shaft like a bandage. I stood back and admired my handiwork. I felt a first glimmer of confidence. First breakage, first repair—successfully accomplished. Maybe I was capable of looking after myself out here after all.

So hah, Mr. Self-Doubt. Bet you didn't think I had it in me, did you!

I looked at the boathook and smiled as I pictured Richard throwing it in the trash. It reminded me of the hard work that had gone into preparing my boat for the race, and the characters that had helped make it happen. As I retired to my cabin for the night, I sent a prayer of thanks winging its way across the darkening waves toward a small, old-fashioned boatbuilders' yard in England.

....

"I have about two weeks' worth of work to be done on a small boat."

It was July 2005 and I was talking to Tim Gilmore in his cluttered, sawdust-coated office in Dolphin Quay Boatyard in Emsworth, a small and pretty village near Portsmouth on England's southern coast. I was renting a quaint, low-ceilinged, four-hundred-year-old cottage on High Street for the summer while I prepared for the Atlantic Rowing Race.

I had just taken delivery of one beautiful silver ocean rowing boat, but she was almost as far from being ocean-ready as she had been when I had first laid eyes on her about eight months previously. It had taken me this long to get the money together to pay for her. I still had three months before she would have to go into a container to be shipped to the Canaries for the start of the race. I was anxious, but not panicking yet—I thought I had plenty of time. I had learned a lot from other ocean rowers about my options for fitting her out and I had a well-defined plan laid out in a spreadsheet.

Originally I had wanted to do most of the work myself to save money and also as part of my drive toward self-sufficiency, but I had to accept that I couldn't learn boatbuilding from scratch and also do everything else that needed to be done before the race start date. I had to choose which was more important: doing it all myself and waiting until 2007 to row the Atlantic, or finding the money to pay a boatbuilder and setting out within the year. Impatience won out, and I decided to delegate much of the boat work.

Even though I wouldn't be doing much of the work myself, I wanted to keep a close eye on things and make sure they were done to my satisfaction, so I was looking for a boatyard near my new home base. In the tiny village of Emsworth my options were limited to two boatyards. Dolphin Quay was the first one I approached.

I walked in off the street, through the gateway in the iron railings and past the old-fashioned sign saying DOLPHIN QUAY BOATYARD, EMSWORTH. TRADITIONAL BOAT SPECIALISTS. I found the office in a dilapidated shed. A miscellany of boat parts, nuts, bolts, and marine catalogs crowded the shelves on one side of the room. Tea mugs stood next to an electric kettle on top of a battered refrigerator. Mismatched chairs surrounded a round wooden table, and a cat snoozed on top of the photocopier. Everything was covered in a fine layer of sawdust, including a bespectacled man in his forties who sat behind the desk.

I introduced myself and stated that I was looking for somebody to help me with my boat, and I deliberately omitted to mention of what kind of boat I was talking about. Since I'd moved to the coastal village of Emsworth I'd learned that most people in the sailing community had never even heard of ocean rowing, and if they had, they regarded ocean rowers as eccentric lunatics. Sailors could not see how anyone in their right mind could resist the temptation to put up a mast and sail.

The man looked nervous, his soulful brown eyes blinking behind his large round glasses. I would soon learn that Tim always looked nervous—or maybe it was only when I was around. He had an earnest manner and a tendency to preface statements with my name—"Roz, errr . . ."—in a way that always made me feel that bad news was coming. Now he just looked quizzical, and I ventured to tell him more.

"My boat isn't exactly a traditional boat," I said, thinking of the sign outside and wondering if this yard was going to be able to help. "It's made of carbon fiber, not wood, and it's an ocean rowing boat." I waited to gauge his reaction.

"An ocean rowing boat?" he repeated.

I braced myself for the customary question, "Are you mad?" generally accompanied by a derisory snort and a hard stare. But Tim caught me off-guard.

"We've worked on one of those before. The *Petrel*. We came up with a new kind of steering system for her. Here, let me have a look for the file."

He rummaged in a drawer and pulled out a file. He walked over to the round table and spread out the contents—an array of technical drawings and photographs, showing a shiny stainless-steel construction of levers and swivels leading to a wooden rudder. The workmanship looked impeccable. I knew I was in the right place.

As time went by I came to appreciate that I couldn't have found myself a better boatyard if I had searched the length and breadth of Britain. Tim chose his senior boatbuilder, Richard Uttley, to do the bulk of the work, with specialists coming in to do the stainless-steel fabrication and finer carpentry. Over the coming months Richard would earn my utmost respect and gratitude. He was a burly bear of a man, with a white beard, a blustery manner, and a phenomenally practical brain. He could convert metric measurements to imperial and back again in a flash, seemingly more by intuition than by calculation, and a problem never survived more than a few minutes in his presence—no sooner would he identify the problem than he would come up with the solution.

The banter between him and the young apprentice, Sam, provided light relief when I was starting to feel the stress of our looming deadline. Richard loved classical music and his radio station of choice was Classic FM. Sam was young and cool and permanently plugged into his iPod to drown out the strains of Vivaldi and Beethoven. Richard would make fun of Sam's girlfriends. Sam would make fun of Richard's age. Of course they loved and respected each other, but either of them would have died sooner than admit it.

Most boatyards are located in marinas or industrial sites. Few are in the center of a village. Dolphin Quay Boatyard was one of these few, which was a mixed blessing. The big advantage was that it was only a few minutes' walk from my rented cottage. At least once a day I would walk the couple of hundred yards along the village high street to the boatyard to see how work was progressing and discuss any issues that had come up.

On the other hand, it could be difficult to work uninterrupted. Passersby would peer in through the open railings that separated the boatyard from the street, and on seeing this strange-looking craft would wander in to ask questions. My most regular visitor was Len, a gentleman in his seventies who always wore a collar and tie and a flat cloth cap. He was thin, with a large, red-veined nose, watery eyes, and a querulous expression. He would drop in about once a week to see how things were going, and was never in a hurry to leave. It was always lovely to see him, but always a relief when he left and I could get back to what I was doing.

Initially work on the boat proceeded without a hitch, but the further we progressed, the more it became apparent that my initial estimate had been ridiculously optimistic. One day we discovered a problem that left Richard uncharacteristically stumped. After much research and lengthy consultation with my ocean rowing mentors, I had decided to buy my oars from a highly reputable Australian company. But when the long-awaited oars finally arrived, and we put the boat in the water and the oars in the oarlocks, we found that the oars were too short. The oar manufacturer had stood on my boat on the river at Henley Regatta earlier that year and confidently declared that oars of 306 centimeters (ten feet) were what I needed, so that is what I had ordered. But here they were now, waving forlornly six inches above the water. Evidently somebody's arithmetic had gone wrong somewhere along the line.

"Errr, we could try raising the Atlantic . . . ?" Richard offered. For days we mulled over the problem. Cut into the side decks? Raise the rowing seat? But for various reasons none of these solutions was practical. Eventually we had to concede that longer oars were the only solution, and after a few urgent phone calls to Australia a fresh consignment of oars was on its way. How these oars would be financed was left vague but the primary concern was whether they would arrive in time.

Time and money were my two constant worries. I didn't have much of either. Looking back now, I have no idea how the cash kept coming, but somehow money always seemed to appear when it was needed. A wealthy friend of a friend contributed £5,000 ($10,000 U.S.) out of his own pocket at an early stage of the project, enabling me to meet the installments on the boat purchase. An online gaming company, ParadiseBet, came in with another £4,500 ($9,000 U.S.) after they heard of me through my chosen charity, The Prince's Trust. Dribs and drabs of funds appeared from friends and strangers alike. I used the remnants of the first installment of my divorce settlement to keep the project rolling while I tried to raise sponsorship.

When I wasn't worrying about money I was worrying about time. It had been a frenetic year. There were many aspects to the challenge and it was a constant struggle to find enough hours in the day to keep chipping away on all fronts. I wasn't sleeping well and would often get up at strange hours of the night to work or train—better to get up and do something than to lie in bed with my mind churning. I was having minor but regular panic attacks at everything that still needed to be done.

Often I felt like Wile E. Coyote, running off the edge of a cliff in pursuit of the Road Runner. His forward momentum would keep him aloft even though his legs were spinning over thin air. All would be well until he looked down and realized the ground had disappeared, at which point he would plummet to the bottom of the canyon. I just tried to keep my legs spinning as fast as possible, resisting the urge to look down. If I could just maintain my forward momentum, keeping my eye on the goal, I hoped that blind faith and optimism would get me to the other side of the abyss.

First among my multitude of worries was the boat itself. No matter how hard I trained or worked at my navigation studies, if my boat weren't ready to go to sea there would be no Atlantic row for me. The summer was ebbing away and, despite Richard's enormous energy and enthusiasm and prodigious work rate, much remained to be done. Two and a half months after we had first met, as we worked late into the night to meet our immovable deadline, Tim Gilmore would wryly remind me of that first time I had walked into the small office of his boatyard with my "two or three weeks" of work.

With just two days left before my boat was due to leave for the race start line in the Canaries, the new set of longer oars had yet to arrive from Australia and the electrical system still wasn't working. The latter was suffering from a committee approach. Three different people had worked on the electronics and now they were all pointing the finger of blame at each other. I didn't know whom to believe, and I didn't care. I just wanted it to work. There would be time to put the finishing touches on the boat once she and I were both in the Canaries, but I was fairly certain I wouldn't have the skills to do anything as technical as fixing the electrical system. Whenever I had a break from training sessions and last-ditch attempts to raise sponsorship, I was to be found prowling around the boatyard, not really helping but too tense to go anywhere else.

I'd tried to be so organized, and yet here we were in a last-minute panic. I didn't even dare think about the money. I had now used the last of my divorce settlement and the sponsorship funds. I knew that the boatyard bill must by now be about £12,000 ($24,000 U.S.) and I didn't know where it was going to come from. Surely fate wouldn't have allowed me to commit so totally to this project, only for me to be thwarted at this late stage by something so relatively trivial as a lack of money. I tossed and turned at night, worrying not only about how I was going to pay, but what would happen if I didn't. Dolphin Quay Boatyard was a small business with little more in the way of financial resources than I had. If I didn't pay my bill on time, I wasn't sure how they would pay the wages. Dark images of starving little Gilmores haunted my dreams.

As it turned out, I should have had more faith. Fortune does indeed favor the bold. The bank agreed to renegotiate my loan to cover the boatyard bill. I may have somewhat exaggerated my level of income (then standing at zero pounds per annum) in order to secure the finance, but the ends seemed to justify the means. Richard Uttley and the electrician worked late into the night to find the loose connection and get the electrical system working. The U.K. agent for the Australian oars drove over to deliver them personally. Their dedication to my project went above and beyond mere professional pride. My row seemed to mean nearly as much to them as it did to me. Fate had tested my nerve by taking me right to the brink before saving me just as I was about to fall over the edge. Money and resources appeared in the nick of time, although not necessarily from the directions I was expecting. It was as if I'd had to put in the hard work, to prove myself willing and dedicated, before the universe rewarded me with the wherewithal to pursue my dream. The lesson I took away from this chapter of my life was: Have faith, hold true to the vision, and work your butt off.

The day of the deadline for shipping arrived and we were busy loading the boat onto her trailer to be towed to the shipping company. It was early in the morning and we were buzzing around in the forecourt of the boatyard making her ready. People were walking by on their way to work. Len dropped by to give me a half-pint glass commemorating the Vendée Globe, a nonstop, round-the-world sailing race for single-handers.

"Oh, Len, that's so kind. You shouldn't have," I exclaimed.

"Oh, it's OK, love, I didn't. They were giving them away in the pub." He patted me on the shoulder and wandered off on his morning stroll around the village. I grinned, amused but also touched.

A few minutes later a woman wearing a brown-checked shop assistant's overall stopped to watch us.

"You're the one I read about in the paper, the woman who's going to row the Atlantic?" she asked me.

"Ye-es," I said, expecting the usual comments ("You're mad") and questions ("What will you eat?" "Where do you sleep?" "How do you go to the toilet?").

Instead she reached into the pocket of her dress and pulled out a ten-pound note.

"I think it's marvelous what you're doing," she said. "I want you to have this. Buy yourself a drink when you get to the other side."

She turned and continued on her way to work, leaving me standing with my mouth hanging open, speechless with gratitude. It wasn't so much the donation that had affected me, as the fact that my crazy adventure meant so much to this total stranger that she had given me what must have been the equivalent of two or three hours of a shop assistant's pay.

The day after my boat had gone into the shipping container bound for the Canaries, I was in the local pub enjoying a pint with the people who had helped make it possible. I told Richard Uttley that I would make sure that their hard work and their faith in me was rewarded, and that I would do my utmost to get *Sedna* and myself safely to the other side of the Atlantic. I gave him a big hug. He blushed, and I thought I saw a tear in his eye.

eight

CLOUDS OF ANXIETY

*t*he wind continued to blow strongly from the south for the next few days. I passed the time alternately between sitting in my cabin, anxiously watching my course on the chartplotter and praying that the sea anchor would stop me being blown too far north, and standing out on deck looking out across the waves, vainly willing the wind to blow the other way. I was glad of the chance to rest my shoulders, and for a valid excuse to take a break from the tedium of rowing, but the forced idleness weighed heavy on me. Activity had helped drown out the negative voices in my head; now that I had too much time on my hands they were running rampant. The skies were overcast and gloomy, as if sympathizing with my state of mind.

On my second day of lying on the sea anchor, I called my mother to find out what was happening elsewhere in the race fleet. She told me that most of the other crews had also been affected by the adverse winds, so I was not losing significant ground. Some of them, my mother told me as she watched the colored blobs moving around on the website map, were suffering greater loss of miles than I was. I was relieved to know I was not the only one in this predicament. Selfish though it may seem, to wish this plight on others, I was anxious to not be left behind.

After I hung up the phone I looked around the cabin and sighed. "Wave after wave of adrenaline-pumping adventure," the race posters had promised. Hah, that's a joke, I thought. I want my money back, and to sue them for misrepresentation. I was so bored. The options for entertainment are somewhat limited when you're sitting on your own in a tiny boat in the middle of an ocean. I picked idly at the skin on my hands. The hard-earned calluses were starting to peel off from the sodden skin, and my feet had turned white and wrinkly. I had been worried about getting sunstroke on the ocean, but at the moment trench foot seemed more likely. I could barely remember what it felt like to be dry and warm.

I opened the hatch of goodies under my bunk and took out a bar of chocolate. Cheer-me-up chocolate, I called it. I hadn't had the opportunity to burn the calories to earn this treat, but a bit of cheering up seemed in order. I seemed to be doing rather a lot of cheering up, though, and my stash of chocolate was diminishing rapidly. I'd better be careful, I thought—if I carried on like this I'd be the only ocean rower in history to actually *gain* weight on the crossing.

Even though there was no rowing going on, it was time to update my logbook. Ship's rules must be observed. I opened up the brown leather notebook and turned on the instruments to get the readings. I frowned at the battery monitor. The state of my two batteries was becoming a major concern. I needed some sunshine to power the solar panels and charge them up, but the sun was not obliging. In an effort to conserve electricity, I hadn't run the water-maker for several days, but now three of my four jerry cans were empty, and I didn't want to break into the water bottles stowed belowdecks because the race rules decreed that crews using their ballast water would incur a time penalty. In previous races some crews had emptied out their reserves of water in order to lighten the boat and hence make it faster. This was dangerous for two reasons. First, the boats were designed to right themselves if they capsized, but only if correctly ballasted. So reducing the amount and hence weight of the water ballast would compromise the self-righting capability of the boat. Second, it was important to have reserve water on board in case the watermaker failed. The water ballast would keep the crew alive until a resupply could be arranged. The bottles had all been sealed with distinctive tape so that it would be obvious if they had been tampered with. The adverse winds were causing me to lose too much time as it was, and I didn't want to fall foul of the time penalty by opening a bottle top. So I decided to run the watermaker for half an hour.

I turned it on and set a jerry can to wait expectantly for the product water, but after a few minutes the pitch of the watermaker's motor started to get lower and lower, until it lapsed into a depressed silence. The battery didn't have enough power in it to keep the watermaker running. I knew it was bad for the batteries to run them this low, and could only pray that they would recover once the sun reemerged from the persistent cloud cover. I put the jerry can away again, only a pathetic inch or two of water sloshing around in the bottom.

The next day, just when it was starting to seem I would be stuck on the sea anchor forever, the wind turned in my favor. So, although the skies were still dark and stormy and the seas were rough, I hauled Sid the sea anchor back on board and started rowing again.

With the wind blowing the "right" way I started to make good mileage that day, even though the conditions were uncomfortable. The harder the wind blew, the faster I would go, but it took every ounce of concentration I had to keep the boat perpendicular to the waves. I found that even a moment's inattention would be harshly punished. *Sedna* would pivot around to lie beam-on to the approaching rollers, and it would take several minutes of one-handed rowing and a lot of swearing to get her back on track. It was like trying to balance the boat on a knife edge. The good news was that because I was being blown so fast I could add little to her speed by rowing hard, so I ended up using the oars more for steering the boat rather than powering her forward. This was a blessed relief to my aching shoulders, which even the three days of forced inactivity had not cured, and I was still relying heavily on painkillers.

While one part of my mind concentrated hard on keeping *Sedna* on course, watching the waves approaching from the stern and keeping her bows pointed dead ahead, another part of my mind wandered back into the past. It returned to a time shortly after my epiphany on the train, and a pivotal episode that had changed the course of my life forever.

....

It was a Saturday morning and I was working in my study when my husband came into the room.

"Rozzie, come here," he said.

"I'm busy," I replied, tapping away at my computer keyboard.

"Come here. Now."

Something in his tone of voice made me stop what I was doing and turn around. He was grim-faced. I followed him into the living room. He handed me a letter and said, "Read this."

I sat down on the sofa, took the laser-printed document from him, and read.

Your Wife—Roz

I would prefer not to be involved and to keep my anonymity but,
as a religious person, and partner of an acquaintance of yours, I have

observed your wife's behavior, and rumors surrounding her, over recent months with increasing sadness. It would appear that she has taken great pleasure in making a cuckold of you.

She has embarked upon a long term love affair with a reasonably well known local man, Tom. This affair has lasted over a year now and started from humble beginnings. I am not in possession of all the facts as Tom himself, who is also a relatively honorable man, closely guards your wife's reputation but their lack of discretion, and obvious affection, has made it common knowledge amongst his acquaintances to whom I am also known, and locals, that they are having an affair. I may be talking out of turn, and this matter has been known to you or tolerated, as it seems unlikely that behavior as brazen as this could have escaped your attention.

It seems that this is not a casual spontaneous fling, but a prolonged, deceitful and planned affair. Although I feel sure that your wife and yourself enjoy a close bond, it would appear that your wife and Tom also care deeply about each other.

My own misgivings are twofold. Although I have no bad feeling toward either man, I strongly disapprove of your wife being maintained in such splendor, thanks to your generosity, yet publicly conducting herself and shaming you in this way. I also know a little of Tom, who is well known for his exterior of brashness which is said to mask a rather sensitive nature. His close confidantes have commented that the strain of conducting this covert relationship, and the obligatory deceit, is having a marked effect on Tom's happiness, and it would appear that neither yourself nor Tom are benefiting from your wife's behavior.

Some people believe that ignorance is bliss. However, I understand that you are a successful man who has worked hard to give your wife her current lifestyle and it seems wrong to me in the eyes of God that she should be behaving this way. I trust that you will forgive me for bringing this matter to your

attention but it seemed unjust to allow you to proceed unaware.
Although I am sure that this information may, initially, reduce the
quality of your married life, I hope that your knowledge of the facts
might enable you to repair matters and, eventually, advance to a
higher quality.
    I pray for you.

A friend.

I read the letter with a growing sense of horror and disbelief. I could not imagine how my guilty secret had been discovered. I hadn't told anybody, and I trusted Tom not to talk, either. We may not have been as circumspect as we should have been about being seen in public, but we'd been careful to avoid places where there was any danger of running into anyone we knew. Had someone been following me? Who had written this incriminating letter? Who could hate me so much as to do this to me?

But putting that aside for now, I had to say something to my husband, who was watching me expectantly. My mind was in turmoil, but suddenly it cleared. The situation had been taken out of my hands. The letter was specific enough to be utterly incriminating. I had no choice but to admit that I was guilty.

"It's true," I confessed.

My husband was unbelievably calm about it. When he spoke, his voice was measured and controlled. "I'm not going to throw you out or anything like that. I just ask that you don't see this man again."

I was overwhelmed by relief. I'd never regarded Tom as a potential replacement for my husband. I'd been looking for someone who would show me love and affection, openly and often, in a way that now rarely seemed to happen at home. I knew my husband and I had something special on a deeper level, something that would always be there, but I was looking for someone to make me happy in a very obvious way, in the present—a relationship of instant gratification. I was grateful beyond belief that this revelation hadn't blown my marriage apart.

I agreed not to see Tom again. And I kept my word—for quite a long time, at least.

But it turned out that Tom was just the symptom, and not the cause of the problem, so avoiding Tom did not make the problem go away—in fact, without Tom to distract me, the deeper issue became more apparent. I started spending long and increasingly frequent sessions in coffee shops, scribbling away in my journal, filling up volume after volume with angst-ridden ramblings as I tried to understand what I was here for, what would make me happy, what was the point of my life?

What did I want? The simplest question in the world, but also the most challenging. My brain just didn't seem to understand the concept. I'd always thought in terms of what I must, should, or ought to do, rather than what I *wanted* to do.

Eventually, in desperation, I took a few days off to be alone in a rented cottage and work my way through a self-help book. I read the advice and completed the exercises, and thought I'd found my answer. I called Tom and told him I wanted to be with him. We resolved to run away overseas, leaving behind our old lives to start afresh.

It didn't work out like that. Bracing myself for his pain, but at the same time full of my own giddy plans for my future with Tom, I told my husband that I planned to leave. I announced I would be moving out the next day. I'd intended it to be a statement of intent, rather than an invitation for discussion, but after eleven years together it wasn't so easy to walk away. He asked me not to go, to take more time to think it over. I'd thought I was certain about leaving, but at that crucial moment I wavered. Now I was being pulled in two different directions by two men, one urging me to leave, one urging me to stay. I was caught in the middle between two powerful personalities. I felt weak, vacillating, confused, no longer sure what to do.

I went to sit on the garden swing to consider my options. I smoked in those days, and so I lit a cigarette with shaking hands, trying to figure it out. I'd just spoken to Tom to tell him that I wasn't going to leave yet, that I needed longer, maybe a month, to think it through before I made a decision. "I can't believe you're doing this," he'd said, frustrated. "You were so certain. Come on, jump. Now. I'm here for you, but I can't wait forever. Do it now. You know it's right." But I didn't know it was right. I no longer knew what was right, what was wrong. And Tom wanted a decision. What I decided in the next five minutes, by the time I finished smoking my cigarette, would determine the course of my entire life, and also my husband's and Tom's lives.

As I swung and smoked, I came to resent Tom's impatience. What kind of love was this, that couldn't wait a few more weeks? If we were going to spend a lifetime together, he should be willing to wait for me. Stubbornly, I decided to stay. I exhaled the last puff of my cigarette in a sigh of relief at having come to a decision. I ground out the cigarette in the hard earth of the flower bed, threw the butt in the trash, and went inside to tell my husband.

For a while my husband and I did our best to resurrect our marriage. We tried to recapture some of the magic we'd had when we first started dating. We went away for romantic weekends, paid attention to each other's needs, and were kind and considerate toward each other. We even started to have fun again. But as I thought more about why I'd been prepared to do something as extreme as leaving my marriage, I realized that it wasn't in fact Tom that I'd wanted, but what he had represented—the opportunity to throw away everything from my old life, my unhappy life, and start over again. When I had written the two versions of my obituary and caught a glimpse of the life I really wanted, I had instantly understood, but not wanted to understand, that fundamental changes would be necessary if I was going to live that life. I had been scared to acknowledge my own infinite potential. So I had tried to pretend that I had never seen that alternative, and went back to the life I had, which although it fell far short of my ideal, was at least reassuringly familiar. But in some remote part of my mind I couldn't forget what I had seen, and I became restless and increasingly miserable as the gulf widened between the life I wanted and the life I had. The affair had been a desperate attempt to avoid confronting the unsettling fact that huge and radical changes were going to be necessary if I was ever going to find true happiness. I had diverted all my pent-up energy—the energy that I should have been directing toward changing my life—into the relationship with Tom.

Reflecting on this as I kept the boat on course, I theorized that maybe I had been so uncomfortable in my life that I had subconsciously been trying to precipitate a crisis as an impetus for change. Tom had represented that opportunity. I had made the mistake of thinking that if only I was with the "right" man, I would be content. That was what I'd absorbed from fairy tales as a child—the princess finds her Prince Charming and they live happily ever after. Now I had realized that real life is not a fairy tale—the truth was that I, and I alone, was responsible for my own happiness. No matter whom I was with, or how he treated me, I could never be happy until I learned to love myself. I couldn't learn to love myself until I knew who I was. And that was something I needed to do alone.

So, with sadness but also with a sense of eager anticipation for the new me that I hoped to find, I told Richard that I was leaving, not for another man, but for myself. This time it was for real.

To anybody else, leaving would have made no sense. I was giving up security, finance, home, love—every last thread of my safety net. But in my heart, I knew there was no other option.

It was the scariest thing I had ever done. Our social circle was made up almost entirely of married couples. Nobody in my family had ever been divorced. I didn't know what life would be like from now on. I didn't know if my parents or friends would still speak to me. I felt I was stepping off the edge of the known world.

The morning after I moved out of our marital home, I woke up and discovered to my faint surprise that the world was still turning. The sun still rose. No bolt from the blue struck me down for having done such a terrible thing. Of course my parents were upset and disappointed. Our friends were surprised and shocked. But over time the hurt subsided. My parents, my friends, and even Richard came to understand my reasons and to forgive me. Inconceivably, the world had not come to an end along with my marriage.

But most importantly, there was an almost instantaneous change in my mental attitude. I'd done something that terrified me and I'd survived. I'd made a difficult decision and acted on it. I'd done something that was far outside my comfort zone. I was impressed with my own courage and determination. The effect on my self-esteem was tremendous and immediate. Now I respected myself. The tumult of anxiety and uncertainty that had preceded my departure was in sharp contrast with the feeling of clarity and serenity that now settled over me. I had made my decision, and I knew there was no going back. I had been stuck on a looping train track, going round and round in circles. Now it was as if I had discovered a lever and used it—I had escaped from the loop and was on a new track leading out into the unknown.

I was now an independent woman alone in the world. For better or worse I had the power to determine my own course without the need for consultation or compromise. I had set myself free to head toward the obituary I really wanted. Whatever befell me from now on, be it success or failure, I would have nobody to praise or blame but myself.

And that, I thought, putting in a gratuitous burst of ten extra-determined rowing strokes that made my shoulders grumble with pain, is why I am here, all alone, in a tiny rowboat in the middle of a rough, hostile ocean. A funny place to look for happiness—but it just might work.

nine

LIFE IS EASIER IN THE STORMS

*t*here is an old sailors' adage that life is easier in the storms, and I found this to be true. My strange ocean existence seemed more tolerable while I had the occasional crisis to divert my thoughts from negative emotions, and keeping myself busy with chores around the boat made me feel I was in control of at least some small aspects of my life. I carefully fanned the ember of self-confidence that I had discovered after the oar repair. I started giving myself an occasional metaphorical pat on the back, rewarding myself with words of encouragement. I found that this self-congratulation had a marvelously restorative effect on my spirits and helped to silence the armchair critics in my head. I couldn't be thinking positive and negative thoughts at the same time. I praised myself to the skies for being tenacious, determined, and disciplined, for carrying on rowing when any sensible person might have retreated to the cabin for the day. The best thing about this technique was that the worse the conditions, the more effective it became. Instead of getting more miserable I actually got more positive, because the rougher the weather the more I could praise myself for my courage and perseverance.

I tried to remind myself of this when, just four days later, I broke another oar. I was doing battle with some unpleasantly large waves. One particularly malevolent wave broadsided me and the downwind oar got caught under the boat. There was an ominous cracking sound as it bent itself around the gunwale. Not good. But it sprung back into shape as soon as I lifted it out of the water, and for a while I thought it might survive.

But as the days went by it became evident that the oar's integrity had been compromised. It was like a straw that had been bent in the middle—although initially it appeared to have recovered from its bending, it now had a weak point and it was only a matter of time before it became useless.

I was less than a sixth of the way across and already halfway through my supply of oars. I could not afford for the attrition to continue at this alarming rate.

After that, whenever I saw a particularly large wave approaching I adopted a brace position: hands down toward my ankles, so the oars were as high in the air and as far out of harm's way as possible. But once in a while there were waves that hadn't read the bit of wave theory that says waves go up and down—they don't actually march across the water. These rogue waves definitely moved laterally, and they meant business. They would come at me like an express train, sweeping in out of nowhere, crashing over the deck, and filling my boat to the gunwales. I would find myself suddenly up to my ankles in water, and while I waited for the brine to drain out through the scuppers I would unleash a torrent of bad language, or sometimes just a depressed sigh, depending on how energetic I was feeling. As the saying goes, depression is just anger without the enthusiasm.

I plowed on through the stormy weather. This was not what I had imagined. Before the race started I had become friends with Dan and Jan, a mother-and-son ocean rowing crew, who had reminisced fondly about gin and tonics at sunset and "Lake Atlantic." This had given the impression that rowing an ocean was the kind of thing that a nice young man and his mother might do, possibly as an alternative to a stroll in the park on a Sunday afternoon. They seemed to have got Atlantic Lite, but I had got Atlantic Hardcore. My growing repertoire of psychological tricks was working some of the time, but at other times I took a nosedive into despondency. My emotional balance tilted nearly as erratically as my boat. Some days my world was a wonderful place—usually when I had figured out a new way to cope with my situation, or had just repaired or improvised something—but other days I wanted to be anywhere else. My bad moods were generally the result of a particular demon getting the better of me—Mr. Self-Doubt and Mr. Self-Critical being especially vocal at this stage—or a poor day's mileage. Even on my best days on the ocean, I was still keen to get to dry land, and the sooner the better. This impatience did me few favors.

On the sixteenth night of the race I was giving myself a hard time. Surely other ocean rowers had endured worse things than a couple of days of bad weather, so I was disappointed that I was not handling it with greater stoicism and fortitude. It seemed I had either underestimated the scale of the challenge or overestimated my ability to handle it. Mr. Self-Critical was rampant, and I was in a thoroughly bad mood. I'd stomped off to my cabin (as much as one can stomp in a distance of three feet on a violently pitching deck), had canceled the evening shift, and hoped that life would look better in the morning.

I awoke the next morning to the sound of silence. No roaring wind, no crashing waves, no rain hammering on the cabin roof. Could it be real? I opened the hatch and peered out. Oh, happy day!

It looked as if my prayers had been answered. There was a break in the clouds, and the dawning sun was beaming pale yellow rays down onto the ocean. It turned into a glorious day of rainbows, light breezes, and plentiful sunshine to power the solar panels. By afternoon the batteries had recovered their charge and the watermaker whirred back into action. I replenished the water reserves in the four ten-liter jerry cans. I had enough electricity to run the iPod for the first time in days and sang along happily (albeit tunelessly) to Simon & Garfunkel. I was able to dry out clothes that had been draped damply around the cabin, making the walls stream with condensation. There was still the occasional downpour, but even those were welcome, cooling my skin and refreshing my mind.

So *Sedna* and I were shipshape and Bristol fashion, and I put in a solid if unspectacular day's rowing. Life seemed to be improving.

But not for long. By five o'clock in the afternoon Sid the sea anchor was out partying again—this was becoming a regular Saturday night occurrence for him—while another big low-pressure system swept across my part of the ocean. It was enough to drive a person insane, these constantly fluctuating conditions, so that just as I felt I was getting into a rhythm the ocean would spring a surprise on me and the rhythm would break down again.

I retired to the cabin and slept for a while, but it was still dark when I woke up. I looked at my watch. It wasn't even midnight yet. I decided to pass some time by posting a dispatch to my website, so I took out my palmtop and stylus and lay down on my bunk to compose the text.

....

It is 10:30 on a Saturday night shortly before Christmas. If I were a normal person I might be in a pub having a drink with some friends. But I happen to be me, and so I am lying alone in a small ocean rowboat about five hundred miles off the west coast of Africa.

The wind is against me, so the sea anchor is out to stop me from being blown backward. I am in my cabin, lying on my bunk. I am cozy, yet not quite comfortable. Lying is less uncomfortable than sitting.

It is sticky and stuffy in here. I've closed the hatch and ventilation holes in case the wind really blows up while I am asleep, so the air comes through a ventilator installed in the round aft hatch above my head. Some nights I can see the moon and stars through this hatch, seeming to dance around in my little window on the sky as the boat pitches and yaws. But not tonight. Tonight it is overcast and dark out there.

There is a faint smell of chocolate and crystallized ginger from my snack packs, stowed in the lockers beneath the floor of the cabin. At first the smell used to make me feel hungry, but now I'm rather sick of it. My mouth is dry—I deliberately allow myself to dehydrate when I know I'll be confined to the cabin for a while, as it's a nuisance having to go out to the rowing cockpit to use the bedpan.

It is noisy in the cabin, but in a soothing kind of way. The structure of the boat creaks and groans. The water laps against the hull, and swirls gurgling around the rudder which is just behind my head. When there is a gap in the gurgling I can hear the sigh of the ocean, and the breath of the wind.

The movement of the boat is different when she is at anchor. She twitches and strains like a terrier at its leash. She seems restless. We rock from left to right, left to right, and occasionally in a circular motion—up and over and around and down. Sometimes we'll get partway through one of these maneuvers when the line to the sea anchor brings us up short, and we're jerked back. And once in a while one of those express train waves will steam in and sideswipe the whole boat through sixty degrees.

I'm not scared. The sea is rough but Sedna *has proved her seaworthiness in worse conditions than this. But I'm not quite relaxed either— even while I sleep my ears are pricked for any unfamiliar sound, any signal that an oar or the rudder or the sea anchor has come to grief.*

It's going to be a long night. I read for a while, then doze, dreaming of Jonah and the whale, then wake up, and it is still only 10:30 P.M. It doesn't get light until 8 A.M. So I'm here, whiling away the time by tapping out my thoughts on my iPaq, its little screen the only light in my darkened cabin. It has just started to rain, pattering down on the aft hatch. I've started to yawn again. Time for another doze. Thoughts blur into daydreams which blend into nightdreams. Time drags on.

....

A few days before Christmas my camping stove broke, condemning me to a cold Christmas dinner. The "breakage" was due to a routine maintenance job combined with human error, and as there were no other humans around it was of course *my* human error.

I had gotten used to using the little camping stove to boil water. I would perform this ritual once a day after my first rowing shift. Some would be used to make porridge and a cup of tea for my breakfast, and the rest poured into a thermos to use later to reconstitute freeze-dried food for lunch and dinner. Before using the stove the fuel canister had to be pressurized by pumping a plunger twenty or so times. The last few times I had used the stove, I noticed that the pump had been losing its effectiveness, slapping uselessly in and out of the cylinder instead of producing a satisfying suction, so it no longer pressurized the fuel effectively and the stove wouldn't light. It needed to be fixed. I was not familiar with this item of equipment, so I got out my file of instruction manuals.

With the sole and rather strange exception of the boathook, I had been obsessive about keeping the weight on board the boat to the absolute minimum—every pound was another pound I had to propel across three thousand miles of ocean—so I had pruned all my instruction booklets down to the few pages that I thought I was most likely to need. I found the few pages I had brought from the camping stove manual and laid them out on my bunk. I squinted at the tiny print.

The text said this was a common problem and what I needed to do was moisten the suction cup. It told me how to take the plunger out of its cylinder, and I would then find the suction cup attached to the end of the plunger. I carefully lined up the arrows according to the instructions, and the plunger came sliding smoothly out of its cylinder. But my sense of satisfaction was short-lived. The suction cup wasn't on the end of the plunger. I peered inside and at the end of the dark tube could just see the cup, stuck in the bottom of the cylinder. I poked around with a paper clip and eventually the cup, a small black cone of rubber, tumbled out. I did as the instructions told me and moistened it with a little saliva. But now I didn't know which way it was supposed to go back onto the plunger.

Unfortunately the page of the instruction manual that showed the expanded view of the stove was one of the pages that I had left behind to save weight. I had a fifty-fifty chance of getting this right. As is usual for a human being faced with such odds, I got it wrong. I put the suction cup on facing the plunger instead of away from it, so when I slotted the plunger back into its cylinder it stuck fast. No matter how hard I pulled, it wouldn't budge.

Maybe it would move once the suction cup dried off a bit, I thought, hopefully. So over the next few days I kept trying it again and again, like a hundred-pound weakling straining at his chest expander, but to no effect. My cooking stove had cooked its last. It seemed cruelly ironic that while my main adversary was one of the biggest entities on the planet—the Atlantic Ocean—my immediate nemesis was a tiny component from a camping stove.

I couldn't help but smile ruefully as I contemplated my five gas lighters. I had been so concerned that they might rust and fail while I was on the ocean that I had brought plenty of spares, and four boxes of matches as well. Now I had plenty of lighters, but nothing to light. If only it were possible to know in advance precisely which bits of kit would fail—a spare stove would have weighed only a few ounces, or the other pages from the instruction manual only a few fractions of an ounce—but I hadn't wanted the extra weight of bringing a spare of everything. That would have weighed, and cost, twice as much. So I had taken my chances, and in this particular case I had guessed wrong and focused on the lighters instead of the stove.

The total stuckness of the plunger had a feeling of finality about it, and within two days of the demise of the camping stove I was fully resigned to my fate of cold food. Even though it was far from ideal, that was just the way things were. I was starting to be impressed with my ability to accept those things that could not be changed, and to adapt to new situations. Although there were some things that I was sure I would never get used to—such as the waves that surged in from nowhere and filled the cockpit—there were other aspects of my existence that I was starting to accept as facts of ocean life. Once I accepted them, they lost much of their capacity to irritate me.

I had mentally moved on and consigned the camping stove to history, but my lack of hot food seemed to be a cause of great consternation to people following my website dispatches. The topic brought forth a considerable number of emails offering advice. One man even gathered a few of his friends and a similar camping stove for a brainstorming session to try and figure out how I could fix it. I was touched by their concern, but to me it seemed a quite unnecessary expenditure of time and energy. I was over it.

Most of my food was still edible in its cold state. Only porridge proved to be unpalatable when raw. For a while I ate a cereal bar for breakfast but this gave me too much of a sugar rush followed by a nauseating sugar crash. One day I tried making some no-cook cookies out of oatmeal and hemp powder. Like a TV chef I assembled the ingredients on the lid of my galley locker. I took one sachet of porridge and one scoop of green hemp powder (which I had brought along as a high-quality, natural protein supplement) and put them in my thermos mug. I added ground ginger and cinnamon for flavoring, and raisins to sweeten the mixture. I added enough water to make a stiff paste and stirred thoroughly, then shaped the resulting green goo into cookies and placed them on a billycan lid to "bake" in the sun. But several hours later the baking process did not seem to have made much difference. They still looked like small green cowpatties. I tentatively took my first mouthful. That first taste was enough to convince me that the experiment had been a complete failure. The "cookies" were soggy and disgusting. Uncooked oatmeal tastes floury and, well, uncooked. I unceremoniously consigned the remainder to the waves, with apologies to any nearby fish hoping for a tasty tidbit.

The next day I devised a more successful recipe: I mixed the hemp powder into a protein sports drink with a teaspoon of coffee. I hadn't drunk coffee since setting out from La Gomera, but I felt the need for something to solve my usual midmorning energy crisis. It seemed to be working well, giving me sustainable energy throughout the morning, although it also necessitated frequent visits to the bedpan as my system adapted to the kick of caffeine.

It was a long way from my ideal breakfast (New York–style French toast, topped with melting butter and maple syrup, liberally sprinkled with cinnamon, served with fresh fruit and ice cream) but it was a good deal better than the hemp cookies.

It wasn't the temperature of my meals that was an issue, but rather their quality and quantity that preoccupied me. By this point in my journey, food was assuming a disproportionate significance in my life. I have always enjoyed good food, having more of an epicurean, live-to-eat kind of approach than a pragmatic, eat-to-live attitude. For me food represented reward, happiness, comfort, and enjoyment.

During my preparation for the race I had consulted several nutritionists about what I should eat during training, and what my diet should be during the row itself. For a number of years it had seemed that if I could get my diet right I could improve my levels of mental and physical energy. In my everyday pre-row life I felt as if I were operating way below my full potential, like a car running with the emergency brake on. I hoped to use the Atlantic row as an opportunity to find the perfect formula for optimal nutrition.

I received lots of advice, but most of it was confusing and contradictory. Everybody had a strong opinion that differed from everybody else's strong opinion. The world seemed to be full of nutritional gurus—people who had found a formula that worked for them and they adamantly believed would work for everybody else. In the course of my research I found the hemp powder guru, the glucosamine guru, and the homeopathic guru. One nutritionist regarded caffeine and sugar as tantamount to the devil's work, while another kick-started his day with two black coffees but wouldn't touch grain or dairy. Some sports scientists advocated formulas full of unpronounceable chemicals, while other experts recommended eating foods as close as possible to their natural state. I was even more confused by the end of my investigations than I had been at the start.

I decided to turn to those who had lived in the real world of endurance expeditions. Most ocean rowers seemed to place more importance on how food tasted, rather than how healthy it was. The usual expedition meals abounded in trans fats and additives, and I knew I wanted none of those. So I turned to the polar explorers—the activity that physiologically seemed to bear the closest resemblance to ocean rowing, since it involves relatively low-intensity exercise for many hours a day over the course of a two- to three-month expedition. It also requires prolific consumption of calories, as does rowing. But the polar people need a diet unusually high in fat to help them combat subzero temperatures, and eating solid blocks of butter was not going to work on the ocean. Foods would go rancid much more quickly on my boat than they would in the high Arctic.

The more I investigated, the more it became apparent to me that beyond a few fundamental principles, every body is different, and each person has to figure out what works for them as an individual. There was no "right" answer to my nutritional questions. To find my optimal blueprint for exercise and nutrition would be largely a matter of listening to my own body and responding to what it was saying.

Ideally, I would have slowly and systematically worked out what was best for me through careful experimentation, methodically eliminating and then reintroducing certain foodstuffs from my diet and gauging whether I felt better, worse, or the same. But in the real world, that was not going to happen. I am not a laboratory rat. During that hectic year of preparation before the Atlantic Rowing Race, meals were often eaten on the fly as I dashed around the country, grabbing whatever was available at highway service stations or on the train. Undeniably there was human weakness as well, and I used the stresses of organizing a major expedition as an excuse to treat myself to sweet, sugary comfort foods.

Although I had not managed to conduct a controlled experiment to find my perfect diet, I had put a lot of thought into what food I would bring with me on my voyage. As well as being tasty and not too expensive, it had to provide a nutritious and well-balanced diet. Tiny Little told me that he had developed scurvy during his one-hundred-plus days at sea, and I wanted to avoid the same fate. Constipation is also a common problem for people on long voyages, since many processed and freeze-dried meals lack sufficient fiber.

I devised a diet that I was fairly confident would work for me. For breakfast, I planned to have porridge or muesli made with powdered milk, with extra nuts, raisins, sultanas, dried apricots, dates, and figs, plus ginger, cinnamon, and brown sugar to add flavor. Lunches and dinners would be based on ready-made freeze-dried meals, but these could be rather stodgy on their own so I had brought sachets of individual freeze-dried ingredients—peas, sweet corn, kidney beans, leeks, prawns, tuna, beef, ham, bacon—and various herbs.

I also had five self-heating meals. These meals took advantage of a heat-producing chemical reaction triggered by water. A sachet of chemicals was in a plastic bag, water was added, and the package was then placed under a boil-in-the-bag meal for twelve minutes until the meal had warmed through. I had only brought five of these because they were expensive and relatively heavy, but they became a highly valued commodity after the demise of my camping stove and I wished I had brought more. I rationed out these precious hot meals to reward myself every five hundred miles, apart from one occasion when I needed a hot poultice to treat an infected finger, so I treated myself to an unscheduled hot dinner and then used the chemical sachet to help draw out the pus from the infection. I was rather proud of this example of lateral thinking—I had not known previously that I could be so good at creative improvisation.

For snacks, I had nut and seed bars with carob topping (called 9Bars), which provided a good balance of protein, carbohydrate, and healthy fats; another kind of bar that the British call flapjacks—made of oats, butter, and sugar, variously flavored with cherries, raisins, hemp, or almonds; and for the sugar-and-caffeine hit that I knew I would crave at night, I had chocolate in various guises—bars of white, milk, and dark chocolate, and chocolate-covered nuts and ginger.

I also had what I regarded as my secret nutritional weapon, an unusual addition to conventional expedition fare. I had gleaned a tip from a book called *The Naked Rower*, about a pair of New Zealanders who had won the first ever Atlantic Rowing Race. They had grown their own bean sprouts on board, to provide a rich source of fiber, vitamins, enzymes, and raw-food goodness. They in turn had apparently gleaned this tip from ancient Chinese mariners. So for the last few months before the rowing race I had been experimenting with various peas and beans, and had found that chickpeas and adzuki beans were the best combination of good flavor and ease of growing. I had several bags of organic beans on board, and a seed sprouter consisting of three stacking trays in which to grow them. After soaking the beans for eight hours or so, I would rinse them in a sieve and place them in the sprouter. Two or three days later, after watering them twice a day, I would have fresh, crunchy bean sprouts that I could eat on their own, or with a splash of soy sauce, or mixed into my dinner or even into my porridge. As well as the nutritional value, there was also a psychological benefit in tending to my own miniature onboard vegetable garden.

This would be the only fresh food I ate during my time on the ocean, with the exception of one supper that, almost literally, fell into my lap.

A few weeks after my stove had failed, I went out on deck for the afternoon rowing shift when something dropped, apparently out of the sky, and landed at my feet.

"Eek" was my first thought (or words to that effect).

Then I saw it was a small but decent-sized flying fish. Many flying fish had landed on my deck before this point, even on one dark night hitting me in the side of the face as I rowed, but they had all been tiny—no more than an inch or so—and not worth eating.

"Supper," was my second thought.

I briefly toyed with the idea of throwing the unfortunate soul back, but he'd injured himself on the inbound flight and was bleeding into *Sedna*'s footwell. I reasoned he was a goner anyway—if I threw him back he'd soon get eaten, and if anybody was going to eat him it might as well be me.

I couldn't bear to hear his death throes, so I took to my rowing seat and sang loudly to myself to cover the sound of the frantically flapping fish in my footwell. Eventually the sounds subsided and I braced myself for the next stage of the operation.

I had never gutted a fish before, and my knife was rather blunt, but it didn't go too badly. I set him on the gunwale of the boat so as to not make a mess on the deck. Then, starting at the tiny hole of his anus (while apologizing to him for the indignity) I slit him along his belly and pulled out the tiny pile of spaghetti-like innards. Then I cut off his head and fins, by which time there wasn't much left of him. Silver scales littered the gunwale, along with a few smears of blood. I rinsed away the evidence with seawater, tied a cord around the fish's tail, and hung him up on the rollbar to dry. I took a photo for my blog of myself alongside my tiny "catch," holding the camera at arm's length. Unlike the pictures of a sports fisherman standing proudly alongside an enormous marlin as big as he is, my catch is almost invisible in the photo, nearly hidden behind the wide brim of my sunhat. But I was excited, and full of anticipation for my fresh fish supper.

Tiny had told me that he had eaten dried fish, but at the time it hadn't occurred to me to ask how long a fish should be dried for. Hours? Days? As I rowed that afternoon I watched his sad little body dangling there, trying to spot any signs of change that may indicate that he was ready to eat, but not much seemed to be happening. I thought if I left him overnight he'd probably get soaked in condensation and go slimy, so toward sunset I unstrung him. His skin had got a bit looser on his body, as if he had lost weight and his skin was now too big for him, so I took this as a sign that he was at least partially dried. I took him in both hands and prepared to eat my first home-dried flying fish. I peeled back the skin from the little corpse and bit in.

The flesh was more sashimi-like than dried, but it was a nice firm texture and tasted good although not strongly flavored. I nibbled delicately along both sides of his body, delicately stripping the flesh from the bones with my front teeth. There was something satisfyingly primeval about eating a fish fresh from the ocean, using nothing but my fingers and teeth. I felt like a true Savage. I declared my first Atlantic fish supper a success, and thankfully I suffered no adverse aftereffects. During my marriage I had been quite the queen of the kitchen, priding myself on serving up tasty and substantial dinners to my husband. Now, looking down at the tiny skeleton, all that remained of my very temporary shipmate, I didn't think that Richard would have been impressed to come home from a hard day's work to find nothing but a five-inch flying fish on his dinner plate.

Many people have asked me before, during, and since my row whether I trailed a fishing line. For a natural mariner this may seem like the obvious thing to do, but for me it was not. With most of my time spent rowing, eating, or sleeping, the time and mess involved in gutting and preparing a fish seemed more trouble than it was worth—especially when there were calories to be had more easily out of a packet. So this one little flying fish was the one and only time that I benefited directly from the fruits of the ocean.

Overall, my food strategy seemed to be working well, and as expedition food goes, it was tasty and nutritious. But there is a good reason that most normal people would not eat freeze-dried food as a matter of choice. Although they gave me what my body needed, my rations didn't always provide what my mind wanted— those psychological feelings of well-being, comfort, and reward.

As time went on, food became the subject of a growing obsession. At night I would dream about sumptuous buffets or dinner parties, and while I rowed I would fantasize about hot buttered toast, or fresh bread with sweetened condensed milk, or rock cakes—the special kind of rock cakes that they used to serve at church coffee mornings that I went to with my parents as a little girl, studded with sultanas and spread with cheap margarine. It was surely no coincidence that the foods I dreamt of reminded me of my childhood. I had long since grown out of such tastes, but now these foods reminded me of easier times. The daydreams were becoming so vivid that I could almost smell the toast, hear the crunch as I bit into it, feel the melted butter ooze out of the bread and coat my tongue with its rich sweetness.

My most bizarre craving was for salted peanuts, something I hadn't eaten for years and had never felt any desire for on dry land. While I'd been stuck on the sea anchor, waiting for the wind to change, I'd been listening to an audio book, Douglas Adams's *The Hitchhiker's Guide to the Galaxy,* in which the heroes supply themselves with bags of salted peanuts just before the destruction of Planet Earth. Peanuts are apparently good for aiding recovery after a leap through time and space to hitch a ride on a passing starship, should you ever need this piece of information. For several days after I listened to that episode, there was nothing in the world that I wanted more than a bag of salted peanuts, something that would have cost me no more than a few pennies on dry land but out here was as unobtainable as moondust. No doubt this utter unavailability contributed to the craving.

After I mentioned in a blog my growing obsession with food, someone texted me to ask what would be my first meal upon arrival in Antigua, and I spent a happy afternoon mentally creating the perfect meal, almost drooling as I rowed. I decided on a large rum cocktail as an aperitif, then a buffet of salads (avocado with buffalo mozzarella and cherry tomatoes, arugula with parmesan and pine nuts, marinated peppers and eggplant, with an assortment of dressings—pesto, lemon, and cilantro, spicy tomato). Then, as the main event, a platter of lobster, served with lime and hot melted butter, crab claws, jumbo shrimp, and barbecued monkfish, all washed down with several glasses of Chablis or a crisp South African Chenin Blanc. Then, if I had any room left for dessert, I would have strawberry shortbread, followed by a caffe latte and three chocolate truffles—one white, one milk, and one dark. It was exquisite torture to imagine the mouthwatering food, the full taste and smell and sensation—but without the calories.

The weather was overcast and for a while I didn't have enough electricity to run my iPod, so I had to entertain myself with my own thoughts—and those thoughts turned ever more to food. I would try to find a rich line of thought that would send my mind off on the longest possible trajectory before it came back to my present situation. I spent most of one afternoon walking the streets of New York, visiting my "happy places"—the old Manhattan haunts that I had got to know when I lived in Greenwich Village for fifteen months in 2000 and 2001 with Richard. In my imagination I meandered around galleries, stores, coffee shops, cocktail bars, blues clubs, restaurants, and nightclubs, conjuring up the tastes and textures of sour cream apple pie à la mode, margaritas, sushi, and BLTs, doing some imaginary Christmas shopping (the best and least expensive kind), ice skating in Central Park, and generally enjoying festive New York. The coffee shop memories were a particular source of delight. My favorite café had been the Cafe Mona Lisa on Bleecker Street. Now I could almost smell the cinnamon of the sour cream apple pie, feel the crunch of the crumble crust, and taste the syrupy tart sweetness of the sliced apples. In my imagination I wrapped my hands around my hot mug of caffe latte, luxuriating in the cozy ambience as I admired the gilded mirrors, the crystal chandeliers, the elegantly faded sofas, and the cute waiter.

But there were many miles and days to go before I would be able to taste my fantasy foods for real (or, indeed, to lust after the cute waiter). I vowed never again to take such pleasures for granted.

ten

HAPPY BIRTHDAY TO ME

*f*riday, December 23, 2005. My thirty-eighth birthday.

I'd hoped to have time to relax and treat myself, although treat myself to *what* I wasn't quite sure. No salons, spas, or movie theaters here. But it looked as if I would be rowing, for time (and tides, and winds) waiteth for no man—or woman.

I wanted to get as far south as possible before Christmas Eve to avoid an adverse weather system—ideally down to twenty-four degrees north, but that would require me to cover a hundred miles in two days, so it seemed a tall order given that my average to date was just over twenty miles a day. This average had been severely dented by a series of days when the wind had been against me. Despite Sid's best efforts, I had been pushed backward by headwinds on three consecutive days immediately before my birthday, logging negative mileage of minus seven, minus ten, and minus three miles. Most days I could console myself with the thought that every mile I rowed was one mile that I would never have to row again, so to find myself faced with a total of twenty miles that had to be re-rowed was demoralizing.

The wind had finally turned in my favor but was due to change again to a southwest headwind the day after my birthday. So if I was going to avoid the third consecutive Saturday night of Sid the sea anchor going out to play, I needed to get a move on and get down to twenty-four degrees of latitude as fast as I could.

As my birthday dawned the wind was behaving impeccably and blowing at ten knots from the northeast. I had been up rowing half the night, so I was hopeful of some good news when BBC Radio Solent rang for one of their regular interviews. This was the local BBC radio station for my last known address, in Emsworth, and during my race preparations, I had become a regular feature on their early morning show. We had continued to speak every couple of weeks since the race started. They always gave me an update on my race position, and I was sure it had to be good news after my overnight effort. I had been ahead of a men's pair, *Move Ahead*, for a while, and had been gaining on another crew, so I hoped I might have moved up a place in the rankings to third from last. When I found out that *Move Ahead* had indeed moved ahead and overtaken me again I was rather crestfallen. I had moved closer to my intended latitude, but it would have been a welcome birthday present to gain a race place rather than lose one.

Radio Solent was having a Christmas party in the breakfast studio and the assembled throng gave a fine rendition of "Happy Birthday" that restored my spirits, as did various birthday greetings sent by email via my website and relayed by Mum.

After that it was down to rowing business as usual, with a special guest appearance that afternoon by a whale. I had been slightly disappointed by the lack of wildlife thus far. People had been texting me to ask what creatures I had seen, but the answer, until my birthday, was diddly-squat. I'd seen no whales, the dolphins were a no-show, and even birds were few and far between. In fact, the only visible wildlife had been a small pink *Homo sapiens* of the Savage variety. This may have been because the waves had generally loomed so large that I could not see far, or because I often zoned out when at the oars, so it was entirely possible that dolphins, sharks, whales, turtles, albatrosses, mermen, and mermaids had been doing triple backflips and dancing the cancan just yards away from me and I hadn't noticed.

The whale made sure I did notice him by blowing loudly to announce his presence. I looked round and saw a pointed dorsal fin and sleek black back arcing through the water about twenty yards away from me. He surfaced and blew a couple more times, and then disappeared from view. Looking in my guide to wildlife of the North Atlantic—so far lamentably underused—I decided he was probably a pilot whale. It was good of him to stop by, and made me feel that this marine environment was not so hostile after all. Because my sightings of marine life had been so rare, the whale seemed to have been specially sent to cheer me up on my birthday.

I had hoped that in the great wilderness of the ocean I would have regular close encounters with dolphins. On my sailing trips their friendly faces and playful antics had never failed to make me smile, but I saw dolphins on just one occasion during my row and that was much later on in the crossing. That day was magical in many ways. It was a perfect day for rowing. The sun was shining, its beams sparkling and glinting off the blue waves, and I was making good progress. Suddenly I spotted the gray back of a dolphin about twenty yards away. As I watched I could see more backs appearing, until there were four or five in the group, and shortly after they had disappeared another group came along, then another, then another. In all there must have been about twenty dolphins, swooping elegantly through the water. They didn't come close—my bow wave presumably being too insignificant to provide a tempting prospect for bow-surfing— but the sight of this marine procession cheered me up immensely. Yet I couldn't quite shake the feeling that the dolphins were mocking me. While I lurched around on deck, confined to my uncomfortable little boat, they exulted in their freedom, leaping gracefully and generally showing off. They seemed almost to be gloating, rubbing in the point that the ocean was their element, not mine.

I also had a couple of turtle encounters. One day I was having a midday nap between rowing shifts when suddenly there was a loud bang on the hull of my boat, waking me with a jolt. What on earth could I have run into out here in the middle of the ocean? I jumped out of my cabin onto the deck and looked around. Nothing. The sound came again. I looked down and there was a big green turtle gazing lugubriously up at me, his wrinkled old head protruding comically from the waves. He hung around for a few minutes, but defied all attempts to take a photograph of him, ducking away beneath the waves every time I took aim with my camera. He exuded a gentle serenity, like a benevolent old grandfather.

Although I rarely saw fish or marine mammals, birds were becoming regular visitors. After the storms of the early days had passed, most days I would see at least one bird, swooping around my little boat, and I would wonder where they had come from and where they were going, and how they would make it there without any food to sustain them. I would often greet them and talk to them, as I would also talk to the boat, the waves, or myself—just to hear the sound of a human voice.

After the birthday whale had departed and I had finished my last rowing shift, I got to the moment I had been looking forward to all day, savoring the sense of anticipation. I went into my cabin and reached into a pocket in the canvas wall-hanging tacked to the wall of my sleeping cabin. I found what I was looking for, and took out the Ziploc bag of homemade greetings cards that my mother had given me before the race started. These were undoubtedly a luxury, but it seemed important to have these little weekly morale boosters. There was one card for each week, to be opened on the Friday. The reason she had chosen Fridays was that my birthday would fall on a Friday, and my birthday was the day that most closely bonded me to her. I had never really thought about this before, but now it struck me as strange that we celebrate birthdays as the achievement of the one who is born rather than the one giving birth. Really, who is the one doing the hard work? So on this particular birthday, for a change, I was celebrating my mother and her contribution to my life, rather than congratulating myself for managing to stay alive for another twelve months.

I pulled out the envelope dated for today, and opened it. The front of the card bore a cross-stitch picture of a red rose, with the words HAPPY BIRTHDAY written in gold above. I pictured my mother sitting in her modest home in Leeds, painstakingly stitching this card, maybe imagining as she sewed how I would feel as I opened it. I knew why she had chosen that particular image. My full name, Rosalind, means "like a rose."

I opened the card to look inside. There, in my mother's distinctive handwriting, uncannily like my own, was written, "To Dear Rosalind, Thinking of you being all on your own on this day. I do hope that some messages get through to you today by other means. Tons of love, Mum." Typical Mum. Not gushy, but totally heartfelt. I could read between the lines and knew that there was love and affection in every syllable.

Feeling rather sentimental, I flicked back through the previous cards she had given me.

An early one: a girl in a kayak with a double-ended paddle, again done in cross-stitch. Inside: "Thinking of you—all the time! And wishing you a good voyage. But I do hope that the oars are long enough! Lots of love, Mum," harking back to the oars-too-short conundrum that had taken place while she was staying with me in Emsworth to help with my race preparations.

Here was another: a small embroidered picture of an approaching liner. "To Rosalind, I wonder whether you have seen many boats or ships? Not unexpectedly I hope. Would be reassuring to know that you are not the only person out there on the vast ocean. Lots of love, Mum."

In these messages I could see all her hopes and fears for me. Although I had no children myself and could only guess at how a mother must feel, I understood that my mother cared, and worried, and felt for me, and that above all she wanted me to be happy.

I was fairly sure, though, that this was not the life she had envisioned for me. By conventional standards, I didn't have much to show for my thirty-eight years—no career, no house, no spouse, no children, not even a car. At an age when most of my contemporaries were settled down to a life of responsible breadwinning and parenting, I was off mucking about on the Atlantic. While most of my mother's friends were knitting baby clothes for grandchildren, my mother was packaging freeze-dried food into weekly ration packs. I silently thanked her for refraining from judgment on my unusual life choices.

As I entered my late thirties I was remarkably unencumbered by possessions or responsibilities. I was free to do what I wished. Selfish? Irresponsible? Some might have said I should be more grown-up, but that was the last thing I wanted to be. To me, it sounded too static. I didn't want to be a grown-up if it meant an end to growing and developing. I wanted to keep a naïve enthusiasm for life, believing that anything is possible. Grown-up. A past participle, as if growing up is something you do once and then it's over. Congratulations, you are a grown-up. Here's your certificate, your cardigan, and your carpet slippers.

I lay in my bunk at midnight that night, listening to the silence of the sea, broken only by the occasional slurp of a wave as it sloshed through the space between the rudder and the hull. It was a peaceful night, and I was experiencing a rare moment of serenity. I reflected on this special birthday and the milestone it represented in my life, and thanked my good fortune that I was here. It may be tough out here, but right now I felt there was nowhere else, and nobody else, that I would rather be.

eleven

ALL I WANT FOR CHRISTMAS

*t*his Christmas would be unlike any other—I could be sure of that. I was not sorry to be spending it out on the ocean, alone. I had not always felt this way about Christmas. I used to love it. When I was a child, as the daughter of good Methodist parents, Christmas meant carols by candlelight, the baby Jesus, and the exchange of gifts around the tree. As I grew older I had looked forward to the office Christmas parties—they meant fewer hours of work—and having an excuse to buy gifts and decorations, and roasting a goose for the in-laws. All had fit well with my focus on material things and my desire to impress. But since the midlife overhaul of my value system the rampant commercialism of Christmas had bothered me, the trees and gift packaging and overeating seeming like an obscene waste of natural resources. The whole occasion had come to seem more and more like a major spending frenzy dressed up in a thin disguise of schmaltz and sentimentality. Now I was grateful for an excuse to avoid the whole overhyped shebang. With my bah-humbug attitude, the middle of the ocean was probably the best place for me to be. Here I could be as Scrooge-like and unsentimental as I wanted.

For the first eighteen years of my life I had been to church every Sunday—a subtle pressure exerted by my parents that while I was living under their roof, that this was how it would be. I hadn't minded at the time. It was simply one of those things, like homework, that I was supposed to do, and it never occurred to me to question it. I didn't especially consider why I went or what it was all about. I barely listened to my father's sermons, allowing his words to wash over me while I gazed around the interior of the church and daydreamed in my materialistic, aspirational way about how I could convert it into a designer home: install a floor to create a loft room under the vaulted wooden ceiling, keep the pulpit as a quaint feature in the living room, create a kitchen in the vestry, sink a swimming pool in the Sunday school hall.

When I went away to college in Oxford, I lapsed. Rather like my relationship with my parents, my relationship with any kind of a God became respectful but distant. Spirituality seemed irrelevant to my life and I stopped going to church.

It had been only since then that I had started to ask what, if anything, might be the purpose of my life and had started to give fresh thought to spiritual matters. I'd had enough of organized religion in my childhood and hadn't found anything there that appealed to me, but I did feel the need for some kind of spiritual dimension to my life. For many years I had worshipped at the altar of materialistic ambition, and now that I had turned my back on money as a guiding principle I needed something else to provide purpose and direction. I needed to evolve my own personal credo.

After much reading and much thought, I had arrived at a personal belief system that worked for me—to my way of thinking it made logical sense and intuitive sense. It was an intensely personal code, not aligned to any of the recognized global religions, and it valued what could be learned through direct experience of life in all its aspects—physical, psychological, and spiritual—rather than what could be learned secondhand through religious scriptures and preachings. I didn't want my faith to be filtered through human interpretation. After so many years of conforming to other people's expectations I had rebelled against being told what to do, how to act, or what to believe—in any aspect of my life. This was partly what brought me out here onto the ocean—I hoped for an intense experience that might prove I was on the right track.

But so far, it wasn't happening.

During my three-month trip to Peru in 2003 I had relied on synchronicity and serendipity to guide me. A kind of magic seemed to pervade my every action there. Things materialized as I wished for them—accommodation, transportion, assistance, and advice. I was encouraged by the experience and hoped to find a similar kind of magic out here on the ocean. On some secret, deep-down level I almost believed I could get myself to Antigua by sheer force of will. I thought that if only I did the right things, for the right reasons, the elements might work in my favor and help me across.

But the ocean was not bending to the power of my will. I was starting to understand why mariners are traditionally superstitious. The ocean seemed so hostile and I was trying all kinds of tricks to coerce it into being more cooperative. When the wind was blowing the right way I would praise the elements, pleading with them to send me more of the same. And when I found myself in the worst of conditions, my instinctive reaction was to ask myself, "What am I doing wrong? What am I supposed to learn from this?" And to believe that if only I could figure out what the lesson was, the wind would change and all would be well again. That was how it worked in the books and movies—the hero aspires, struggles, gains enlightenment, the fates relent, and he achieves his goal. The music segues from dramatic to upbeat, and everybody lives happily ever after. But my story seemed to have a different scriptwriter. From time to time I would have an "a-ha" moment, when an insight would occur and I would dash off to my logbook to note it down, hoping that this was the magic spell that would change my fortunes. But it wasn't working. The ocean seemed to be an amoral and atheistic place. No matter what I did, the ocean simply carried on doing what oceans do, obeying the laws of physics, caring nothing about me and my hopes and dreams. I had never felt so utterly insignificant, so unable to control my environment, so totally ignored. Eventually I grudgingly accepted that there was no way I could influence the wind and the waves by intention alone, and the only way I was going to get to Antigua was stroke by repetitious stroke.

Christmas Day itself proved to be especially trying. Of all the latitudes, in all the oceans, in all the world, I'd had to pick this one. It seemed that I, and I alone out of all the race fleet, had found myself a uniquely unhelpful weather system. The wind was blowing the wrong way—the wrong way for my purposes, anyway. Christmas morning brought the news that I had dropped another race position, and that the winds would be against me all day.

For several hours in the morning I valiantly but grumpily battled the headwinds, rowing hard just to stand still, nearly crying with frustration as time after time the fickle wind would change direction so in the space of a few strokes I'd find myself pointing completely the wrong way. The best course I could make was a very slow west-northwest, which might get me somewhere but certainly not Antigua. "Happy bloody Christmas," I thought to myself.

Exhausted and fed up, I took a break to power up the palm-top and check my emails. One was the three-day weather forecast, showing much more favorable winds starting tomorrow. This put a different perspective on the day. Rather than row myself into an oblivion of misery and exhaustion, I decided to enjoy Christmas and get back to racing when conditions were better. I stowed my oars, put Sid the sea anchor out to play, and made plans to wash my hair.

But first I had some housekeeping to do. It was time to scrub barnacles off the hull of my boat, which would involve going over the side for the first time. I had been advised to scrub the hull every couple of weeks, but the conditions so far had been too stormy and scary. I was distinctly apprehensive, unnerved by the thought that the ocean was over two miles deep. Trapped as I may have felt in the restricted world of my boat, *Sedna* and I were much safer together than apart. Also, I knew that there were sharks in this part of the Atlantic, and I was worried that I might become too exhausted and be unable to climb quickly back on board over the high sides of my boat should a predator show up.

My nerves were threatening to get the better of me, so I briskly put on my mask, snorkel, and safety harness and hopped into the water before I had a chance to think of any more reasons not to.

As usual, it turned out that the anticipation had been much worse than the reality. As soon as my naked body slipped beneath the waves I felt a sense of calm come over me. Looking down through the water, I was mesmerized by its beauty—cool, blue, and limitless.

I had envisaged perhaps a whole colony of wildlife living under my boat, as I had heard that even the smallest craft becomes a congregating point for sea creatures, so I was faintly disappointed to see that there wasn't much at all. There were a couple of tiny little stripy fish, and farther down hovering around the rope of the sea anchor was a bigger fish, maybe a tuna. Apart from that it was just clear blue infinity.

I took the scouring pad that I had strapped to my wrist and worked my way around the hull of the boat, scrubbing at the stunted barnacles that sprouted beneath the waterline. Even though the water was relatively calm, the movement of the boat in the waves brought the hull swinging down dangerously toward my head as I worked. I clung on to the yellow grablines and tried to avoid being either lacerated by the sharp barnacle shells or knocked unconscious by the bouncing hull. The water swirled noisily in my ears and my heart was pounding.

Beautiful though the underwater foray had been, it was with a sense of relief that I clambered awkwardly back on board when the job was done. Now it was time to wash my hair for the first time since the race had started. My body was acceptably clean, as I had been bathing regularly with a sponge or wet wipes, but my hair had generally been stuffed under a hat and left to its own devices.

For half an hour I sat on deck, feeling like a mermaid as I carefully combed out the knots from my tresses. It felt astonishingly good to get rid of all the tangles. I shampooed and conditioned—using organic products so as to minimize contamination of the ocean when it came to emptying the water bucket overboard. It was an awkward process. I knelt on the rolling deck and hung my head down over the bucket, pouring water over my hair using a measuring jug. Then I bathed with a bucketful of fresh water, rinsed out some salty clothes (which was my version of doing laundry), cleaned the boat, and settled down to a Christmas dinner of chicken with cranberries, peas, sweet corn, and gravy. It wasn't bad, but maybe not as good as it sounds—the chicken was diced and freeze-dried, mixed into a kind of Christmas soup with the other ingredients in my thermos flask. The lack of a camping stove meant that it had to be eaten cold, so it definitely lacked the warm comfort of a proper Christmas dinner. This was followed by the homemade Christmas pudding that Tiny had given me, served with Irish coffee–flavored syrup and sweetened condensed milk.

I rang a few people, including my mother and sister, who were celebrating Christmas together at Mum's house in Leeds.

It was now the second Christmas since Dad died, and a bit of a strange one, with me being on the ocean and my sister about to set off on a one-year trip around the world. None of us felt especially festive.

So all in all it was a rather strange but very satisfactory Christmas Day—my main complaint being that Santa had failed to deliver the one thing I *really* wanted for Christmas, which was a nice steady northeasterly wind.

twelve

ROGUE WAVE RUMBLE

a few nights after Christmas, I was rudely awakened when, without warning, a huge wave slammed into the side of the boat and tipped her onto her side. My semiconscious body lifted off the thin mattress and bounced off the canvas lee cloth that formed a vertical wall alongside my bunk.

I flew through the air like a rag doll in a washing machine, limbs flailing as assorted possessions and I flew around inside the rotating boat. Saltwater poured in through the ventilation hatch above my bunk, onto my sleep-fuddled head. I felt like I'd been woken by a particularly brutal sergeant major upending my mattress and throwing a bucket of cold water in my face.

"What the . . . ?"

I had been deeply asleep in the unusually calm night, being rocked by gentle swells when a rogue wave had turned my world upside down. When the boat and I righted ourselves, I turned on the cabin light and assessed the damage. So far I'd managed to keep my bunk remarkably dry and salt-free, but now it was no longer so. Sleeping bag, pillow, and blanket were all sopping.

This was not a good start to the day. My bunk was my haven

and my refuge from the wet, salty world outside. At the end of each shift I'd crawled gratefully into my cabin to curl up on my mattress for a nap, a welcome respite from the relentless harshness of my current living situation. I looked forward to my naps with enthusiasm, wishing myself sweet dreams as I lapsed gratefully into sleep. Now my haven was drenched and would be impossible to get properly dry again, as the residual salt in the bedding would absorb even the slightest bit of moisture from the air.

In the small area between my bunk and the exit hatch, the living area (all three square feet of it) was in total disarray. Everything that had been on the right side of my cabin was now on the left. The crate of food was wedged against the instrument panel, and Monty, the teddy bear, had plunged head-down into the sachets of freeze-dried food and snack bars, only his two little back paws visible. It was a particularly undignified pose for any self-respecting bear.

I'd set out from the Canaries with everything stowed securely, tethered with stretchy cords or tucked into pockets, but as time had gone on my standards had slipped. Life on a constantly pitching boat was hard, with even the simplest tasks taking double the effort and four times the time. I was always having to brace myself or hang on to a handrail to keep myself from falling. It was inconvenient to untie things before using them and then tie them down again afterward, so little by little I'd grown sloppy. This scene of chaos was the result.

"Slob," chimed Mr. Self-Critical.

I'd have to sort it out later. I needed to get out on deck to find out what was happening there.

I hastily pushed aside the clutter of objects that was blocking my way to the hatch, turned the levers, and pushed the hatch open. The moonlight revealed a deck awash with water, slowly draining out through the scuppers. It must have been one heck of a wave.

I conducted a quick survey of the situation. Disaster. Beyond the flooded footwell immediately in front of me, the spoon of an oar lay disembodied on the deck. Better put it somewhere safe before another wave came along and washed it away. I may yet be able to reattach it. I threw it into the cabin behind me and quickly slammed the hatch shut for safety.

I looked up to check on the rest of the oars, stowed diagonally across each side of the boat, from the gunwale at the bow to the rollbar on the roof of my sleeping cabin at the other. Two of my oars were already broken. I hoped that the severed spoon might be from one of the already-broken oars.

No such luck. I could see a stunted shaft where the disembodied spoon had broken away—and it was one of the previously intact oars I'd been using to row with. Now that oar was nothing more than a useless stick. Even worse, the other oar that I'd been using had almost lost its spoon, too. The hollow tube of the shaft was broken almost all the way around, and the spoon hung on by just a thin thread of carbon fiber. Out of the four oars I had set out with, all of them were now damaged: one was cracked in the middle and currently in use as a guardrail; the second was bent in the middle and had lost its integrity; the third had lost its spoon completely; and the fourth was almost spoonless. I was less than halfway across the Atlantic, and already all my oars were broken.

The ocean was proving to be a very challenging opponent. I had known she would be. But so far most of her moves had been tentative little jabs and playful punches compared with this full-on attack on my oars. Without oars I would be adrift on the ocean with no means of propulsion. It might be possible to call on one of the support yachts to bring me replacements, but if I accepted physical help I would lose my unsupported status. I might have been one of the slowest rowers in the race, but I regarded my self-sufficiency as sacred. One of my main objectives in embarking on this adventure was to prove that I could do something by myself, without assistance, and I was fiercely protective of my independence. I would do almost anything to maintain it. I would just have to find a way to repair my oars using what I had on board the boat.

I would tackle that particular job at first light. For now there was nothing to be done but retreat to my cabin and feel sorry for myself. I climbed in and closed the hatch behind me.

The wind was still blowing powerfully the next day as I set about my task. This was helpful in some ways because it meant that even while I was carrying out these necessary repairs, I was still making healthy progress, blown along by the gusts. But it also meant that everything took much longer than it would have done on dry land because the constant rolling of the boat made it difficult to do anything with precision. Everything had to be carefully put in a safe place or else it would roll away across the deck, or get swept away by a wave. I took the remaining section of the telescopic boathook and flattened out the end with a hammer. This was not easy—the hammer kept glancing off the smooth metal as the boat lurched from side to side—but eventually I had my splint. I lashed the unflattened end to the shaft of the oar, and then tried using glue to fix the flat section to the spoon of the oar.

The instructions on the pack of the glue tube told me that both surfaces to be glued "must be clean and dry." By now there was almost nothing on my boat that was either clean or dry, much less both. Both the splint and the spoon were salty and wet, and I could not keep them otherwise for long enough to complete the gluing operation. I thought of trying to screw the spoon of the oar to the splint, but I couldn't manage to drill through either the pole or the center of the spoon—they were both too hard and the drill bit just skittered off to the side. After struggling for a while I found that only the center section of the spoon was too hard to drill—the sides were softer. So I drilled two holes through these softer sections and used cable ties to secure the boathook to the back of the spoon. The resulting oar was unbalanced and uncomfortable to use, but it worked—just about.

I needed another oar to make a working pair, so the first broken oar was relieved of guardrail duties and restored to active duty. I had already splinted it with the first section of the boathook, so I reinforced the repair with extra duct tape, binding it tightly to make the repair as strong as possible.

The repairs had taken me the best part of a day, but the day had been productive in more ways than one. When I checked my GPS, I discovered that I had logged one of my best daily mileages to date. I had covered over thirty miles without rowing a single stroke. "Good job!" "Keep up the good work!" came the texts when I turned on the phone that evening. Life is strange, I reflected as I scanned through them. I slog along for days with little reward, then I stop rowing altogether and start whizzing along. I was used to a world where effort and results went hand in hand. But here on the ocean, the rules were different.

The next morning, when I turned on my satphone, I received a text from a friend who was a senior officer in the Royal Navy and wanted to know if I shared his passion for the high seas. "Have you fallen in love with the ocean yet?" he asked. I snorted. Easy for him to love the ocean, from the relative comfort of a navy destroyer with a crew of two hundred men, hot food, and hot showers. Less easy for me to love the ocean, when she seemed to have made it her mission to make my life a misery.

Living on the south coast the previous summer I had met lots of people who genuinely did love the sea and couldn't wait for the next opportunity to go sailing, cruising, or just messing about on the water. I could occasionally see why many people love the ocean—she and I had a few rare but magical moments, as I rowed quietly on a calm moonlit sea, or surfed along on rolling blue waves, or watched the setting sun sink into golden waters—but more often I saw the nasty side of her nature—the scary stormy waves, the spiteful little breaker that came along and soaked me just as I was about to retire to my bunk, the occasional hit-and-run wave that would knock me down and race off without a word of apology. It was hard not to take this abuse personally. The ocean seemed to be trying to break my will, and although she hadn't yet succeeded, she had been close.

John Fairfax, an ocean rower in the 1970s, got so annoyed with the ocean that in a magnificently futile gesture he had fired his harpoon into the waves. I hadn't yet reached that height of fury, but I could totally understand his frustration and his need to vent it in some active way. I don't normally feel the need to express anger physically, but when my sister and I were little she would sometimes get me so wound up and angry that my hands would bunch into involuntary fists, itching to hit her—which of course I would never have done, but the red mist was almost overwhelming. And similarly, and only occasionally, during my marriage I would sometimes get so annoyed with my husband that I would have to go and take it out on the dirty laundry pile, kicking sweaty gym kit and underwear into the air until I had calmed down.

But here on the boat there were no easy targets on which to exorcise my frustrations without breaking something important or hurting myself. So I had to limit myself to purely verbal methods of venting my spleen, and *Sedna* had witnessed some full and frank expressions of opinion directed at the ocean.

There were times when she seemed to be downright malicious, timing to perfection the moment to strike so as to cause maximum inconvenience. Her favorite trick was to swamp me just as I sat down to eat dinner. When I still had the ability to heat water it would take about ten minutes to rehydrate my dinner, but now it took three or four hours to rehydrate in cold water. So I had to set my dinner to soak well in advance of mealtimes, mixing the ingredients in a mug, adding water, fitting the lid, and placing it safely in the mug holder on the bulkhead in front of me. My hunger would grow as I rowed, and I would stare at the mug, anticipating the time when my dinner would be ready to eat. The hours passed slowly. At last I would finish my rowing shift, leaving the rowing seat to sit on the hatch lid by the footwell. Ah, blissful change of position. I would stretch my back. Then, eager with anticipation, I would retrieve my spoon from the D-ring on the deck where I normally left it for convenience. I would lift the mug from its holder, and remove the lid. Saliva glands would be working overtime, spoon poised . . .

The ocean knew. She knew that now would be the exact time to strike. The wave would come, sluicing over me, running down the back of my waterproof top, swamping my dinner in salty, cold, spiteful water. It would take too long to prepare another meal, so I would eat my watery dinner, cursing the ocean with every mouthful.

The ocean was also taking a toll on my electronics. A few days before the breakage of my last two oars, my precious music system had died. I had been using an ordinary car stereo to transmit the music from my iPod, trusting to the watertight integrity of my sleeping cabin to keep it sufficiently dry. But as I should have learned from my sailing experiences, seawater gets everywhere. Condensation and water had made their way into the cabin and the dampness had clearly proved too much for the amplifier. Its display had started to blink, and after that it entered a rapid decline. A few days later, with a few dying flickers of its display it followed my camping stove onto the list of casualties. I could have put my music player in a waterproof case and listened to it through headphones, but I've never liked wearing headphones because they make me feel insulated from the world, and no matter how harsh that world, I prefer to be living in it than cocooned from it. So now I had nothing to listen to but the sound of the wind and the waves, and nothing but my own thoughts to keep me amused. My thoughts could be quite entertaining, but I wasn't sure for how long. I feared I might run out of thoughts to think before I reached the other side of the ocean. I became increasingly introspective, for hours at a time existing only in the space between my ears—and at times it could get very crowded in there with the disagreeable company of Messrs. Self-Doubt, Self-Critical, and Competitive. With no external stimulus, my thoughts often became self-destructive.

One day a text arrived that highlighted the contrast between my perception of my situation and how it was seen from dry land. A former ocean rower sent a message saying, "Enjoy this freedom while you can. You will never be this free again."

Free? I thought indignantly. *Free?*

A funny kind of freedom. Free to do anything I want, so long as it could be done alone, on a twenty-four-foot rowboat, in the middle of an ocean. I was feeling far from free; in fact, I had never felt so trapped. I had got myself into a situation from which there was only one way out—and that was to carry on rowing.

I started to wonder what kind of life the sender of that text must have, to regard my current life as free. I realized that over the preceding years, since I had opted out of what most people regard as "real" life—jobs, mortgages, bills, possessions, and obligations— I had reengineered my life so that it gave me an unusual degree of freedom. By not wanting a home or material possessions I didn't need to have a regular income. By having no fixed abode I could go wherever the whim took me. By not having one special relationship I could do what I wanted, when I wanted. I had almost total freedom of choice.

I had hoped to find an even greater degree of freedom out on the ocean. I wanted to be free of time constraints, of people's expectations, of the hustle and bustle of twenty-first-century life.

In the wide-open spaces of the ocean I had hoped to find an escape from the mental clutter of daily existence, and in that extra head-space find some kind of enlightenment. This was supposed to be an oceanic retreat, an opportunity to contemplate life from the outside, and from that perspective gain fresh insight.

But the things that I had hoped to escape from were still taking up a disproportionate amount of room in my head. As well as intrusive banalities and trivialities, there had been some larger issues, problems, and awkward relationships that I had hoped to leave behind on dry land rather than tackling head on. But they were still haunting me out here on the ocean. I realized that I could try and run away from life, but it would still track me down and find me. If I was truly enlightened, I could be as free in a crowded room as in the middle of the ocean. And if I wasn't, I could feel as trapped in the middle of the ocean as in a prison cell.

So, did I love the ocean?

Strangely, despite all the horrible things she was doing to me, she did have her redeeming features. I loved the solitude, the wildness, the beauty. But the ocean and I would have got along better if she would stop trying to get in the boat with me. And if she weren't quite so awesomely, overwhelmingly, big.

Since my stereo had broken I often found that a tune would get stuck in my head for days on end, repeating itself endlessly until it drove me crazy. The tune that had been playing on my mental jukebox for several days now was by U2:

Now you're stuck in a moment
And you can't get out of it

That was exactly how I felt. Stuck. Stuck here in this little boat hundreds of miles from anybody. Stuck with a load of broken oars. Stuck in pain with cold food and no music until I get to Antigua.

If only I could take a break, to somehow escape the confines of this claustrophobic boat it would have been easier to bear, but I couldn't take an evening off from it and head down to the pub with my mates for a few beers and then come back refreshed. It was just me and this big blue ocean, day after day, until I had rowed every last mile of it. I had got myself into this situation and now I had to row my way out of it.

I was impatient to get this ordeal over and done with, but my impatience was only making life harder. The ocean does not respect ambition or schedules—the only way for me to get to Antigua sooner rather than later was to row more hours in the day, and the extra burden of my self-imposed deadline weighed heavily. Lack of sleep and endless days of toiling across the sea were taking their toll on morale. I was utterly fed up.

I would often come to a point in my rowing shift where the boredom, discomfort, and frustration would reach a tipping point, and I would swear loudly to myself and throw the oar handles down in disgust. Then I would remind myself that I had to keep going and I'd take them up again, only to give up again a few strokes later. I was falling apart. It wasn't physical fatigue. I simply couldn't find the mental strength to keep going. My frustration was building to a boiling point. Something had to change or I would explode.

That night, to my shame, I had a little weep on the phone to my mother. I was ashamed, not because there was any shortage of reasons to cry, but because I had chosen to do this row of my own free will, and if I was finding it harder than I ever imagined I had only myself to blame.

A few days after the rogue wave the weather improved slightly, the oars were as repaired as they could be, given limited materials and skills, and I had started rowing again. But my spirits were still in the doldrums. I stood up at the end of my first rowing shift

My mother, Rita Savage, with me aged 2 weeks (1968).

My father, Hamer
Savage (1965).

Rowing with the Oxford University Women's Lightweight squad.

Training for the Atlantic on my WaterRower.

With my boatbuilder, Richard Uttley.

Mum packing food for the voyage.

The start of the Atlantic Rowing Race, in La Gomera in the Canary Islands.

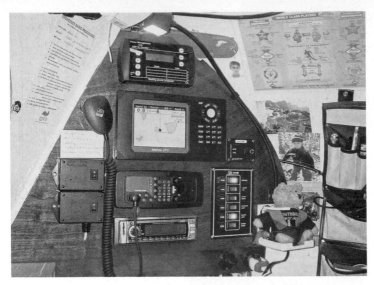

Sedna's control panel, showing chartplotter, Sea-me radar enhancer, VHF radio, stereo, and switch panel.

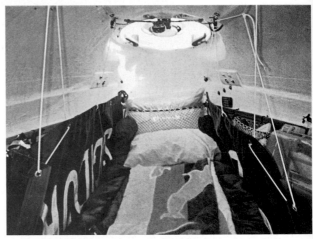

My bunk in *Sedna*'s cabin.

Dinner.

My vegetable patch—growing my own bean sprouts.

Rowing.

Rough seas.

Self-portrait.

Blisters and calluses.

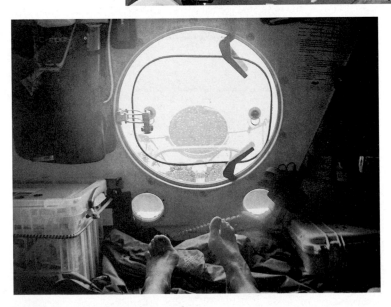

Broken oar number 2.

Killing time while on sea anchor.

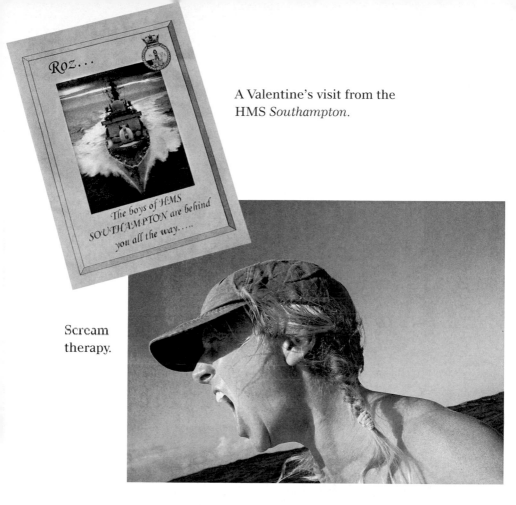

Roz...

The boys of HMS SOUTHAMPTON are behind you all the way.....

A Valentine's visit from the HMS *Southampton*.

Scream therapy.

The Hug—an emotional reunion with my mother in Antigua.

Twenty-five pounds lighter.

Relaxing in Antigua.

and looked over the side of the boat. Rays of rare sunlight created an illusion of a tunnel leading down, down into the blue depths. It was mesmerizing. Tiny motes drifted through the sunbeams, catching the light and sparkling seductively. As a child I'd had many dreams of drowning—dreams, not nightmares, of looking up through blue waters to the sunlight above while I sank to sweet oblivion. It would be so easy just to slip over the side into the cool water and drift down that sparkling tunnel, the waves closing over my head as I slowly surrendered myself to the ocean.

My eyes widened and glazed over as I imagined the release, an end to my struggles. So easy . . .

I shook myself and grasped the guardrail firmly. That was not the way I was going to get out of this situation. I might be struggling and full of self-doubt at this moment, but this moment would pass. I felt so low, the only way had to be up. If not for my own sake, then I had to carry on for the sake of all the people who had helped me get here—the boatbuilders, supporters, sponsors, well-wishers, and friends who had shown such faith in me. If they believed in me, it was not for me to let them down. I thought of my mother, and her grief over my father's death just eighteen months ago. An image flashed across my mind of her anguished reaction if I were lost at sea. I couldn't do that to her. I would get out of this alive. I would carry on rowing, and row back to life.

And luckily, just when I needed it, I got a little help from my friends. The satellite phone beeped to signal an incoming text message.

A former competitor in the Atlantic Rowing Race, whom I had met a few months previously and who had been following my increasingly somber blog entries, had written, "When nothing else seems to work, go to the bow of the boat, take a deep breath, and yell. You will be amazed by the results."

Normally I was not given to yelling—voices were never raised in my family when I was growing up, and even now loud voices could give me an adrenaline surge of anxiety—but I had nothing to lose by giving it a try.

Feeling a bit foolish, even though there was nobody within several hundred miles to see my bizarre behavior, I stood up on the deck in front of the hatch to the aft cabin. This was the only place on board where I felt safe to stand, as I could hold on to the rollbar mounted on the cabin roof, from which my various antennae and aerials sprouted. It was a bright and sunny day and I was already naked apart from my baseball hat. With my arms extended down backward from my shoulders I gripped the bar and straddled the footwell. I sucked in a lungful of air and braced myself.

"Aaaaaaarrrrgggghhhhhhh!" I bellowed, my neck straining forward as I emptied my lungs. I fixed the blue ocean with a hostile glare and directed all my angry energy its way. *So what do you think of that, you useless puddle of water!?* The waves lapped around *Sedna*'s hull, mute and unresponsive.

"AAAAAAAARRRRGGGGGGGGGHHHHH!" *Hah, take that!*

"AAAAAAAARRRRRRRRRGGGGGGGGGHHHHHHH!" *I hate you I hate you I hate you I hate you!*

"AAAAAAAARRRRRRRRGGGGGGGGGHHHHHHHH!" *Can't you give me a helping hand, you bastard? Would it really hurt, just a little push in the right direction?*

I yelled. I ranted, I raved, I begged. I dredged up all my frustration and fury—at the ocean, at the weather, at myself for having gotten myself into this stupid situation—and bellowed it out from the pit of my soul until my throat hurt and I could bellow no more. All my pent-up anger was spent. I felt exhausted but cleansed. It had been a cathartic experience. The ocean, of course, carried on doing what it usually did, with a total lack of regard for any puny little human jumping up and down on the deck of her boat and swearing at it. But my yelling session had made me feel better. I was coming to appreciate that my reality here was largely a creation of my own mind, so if I could adopt a positive attitude, then the ocean could do what it damn well pleased and I could still be happy in my own private version of reality.

In that moment, a surge of realization washed over me. Here I was, struggling and uncomfortable, but *this is what I wished for!*

When I was preparing for this, every time someone asked me why I was doing it, I said I wanted to get out of my comfort zone. And getting outside my comfort zone is, by definition, going to be uncomfortable! Being uncomfortable doesn't mean I'm failing—it means I'm succeeding!

The impact of the epiphany caused me to lose my grip on the rollbar and I lost my balance. I nearly tumbled headfirst into the water but I regained my handhold just in time, and considered this startling new discovery. My stated objective had indeed been to move outside the sphere of what was known and comfortable, and to put myself in a new and challenging situation. I had wanted to get out into the strange and unfamiliar territory of the unknown. That was where I was now, in the *discomfort* zone. This was the realm of infinite potential, where anything was possible if only I had the courage to persevere with it. If I could find the strength to stay out here in the zone of my discomfort, eventually my bubble of comfort would expand and catch up with me. Its boundary would extend to include this place which right now felt so new and scary. Given enough time and repetition, the uncomfortable would become comfortable, and I would have achieved my objective.

Until now I had not appreciated that the discomfort was an integral and necessary part of the process, but now I could see my situation from a different perspective. I perceived that discomfort was actually my friend, because it meant that I was on the right track. I recalled how my muscles used to feel after the first heavy weights session of a new rowing season. My thigh muscles would be so tight and sore that I would have to walk down stairs sideways. But I loved the feeling, because it meant I had pushed myself, and I knew that with more training and adequate recovery the pain would lead to stronger, fitter muscles and improved performance. What I had been going through over the last few weeks was exactly the same, except the pain had been mostly in my mind, not my body. If I could manage to persevere with my mental training, painful though it may be now, my reward would be a stronger, fitter mind, capable of taking on even bigger challenges.

I went back to the oars with renewed energy, if not enthusiasm. I gave myself permission to be miserable and positively rejoiced in my litany of complaints—oars broken, food cold, shoulders aching, boil on bum, stereo not working, etc. etc. etc.—because my level of discomfort was in direct proportion to the distance outside my comfort zone, and the further I was out there, the more I was growing.

Whether I was enjoying the experience or not became blissfully irrelevant, and I spent the rest of my rowing shift cheerfully hating every moment.

thirteen

GOING GARBO

Shortly before New Year I had a visit from the support yacht *Aurora*. That morning my mother, looking at the Woodvale race map, tipped me off that the red blob representing *Aurora* was approaching the purple blob that represented me, and I guessed I was about to receive visitors.

The prospect made me grumpy. Despite it being the festive season, I was feeling distinctly antisocial, and did not welcome this unrequested intrusion. I had got rather used to being the only person as far as the eye could see, and I didn't welcome trespassers on my bit of ocean. I resentfully dug out some shorts and a T-shirt to make myself presentable, having been rowing buck naked for some time now. It felt strange to be wearing clothes, and the slippery Lycra shorts meant I kept sliding off the alpaca-skin cover of my rowing seat.

I kept a lookout for their white sail, knowing that it would be a lot easier for me to see a hundred-foot mast than for them to see my tiny silver boat, hidden among the waves, but I couldn't help hoping that they wouldn't find me. It was a bright and breezy day, and I kept mistaking the white foaming crests of breaking waves for a sail. Every time I realized it was a false alarm, I felt a sense of relief.

At last I saw what was undeniably a sailing yacht, and somewhat reluctantly hailed them on the VHF marine radio. The crew member who picked up my call was my friend Dan Byles, who had rowed the Atlantic with his mother, Jan, in the first ever Atlantic rowing race in 1997.

"Hey, Dan," I called across the VHF airwaves, "I've got a bone to pick with you. You told me you and your mother called this Lake Atlantic, but it's been horrible out here. Roughest lake I've ever been on."

"Yeee-ess," he replied. "Been a bit of a nasty year. But you seem to be going well. You're looking confident and rowing strongly."

"Yep, I'm feeling good," I claimed with fake cheer. It was half true. My shoulders still hurt and I still had a boil on my bottom, but there were some bits of me that didn't hurt so much, so it could be truly said that at least some parts of me were feeling good.

Dan came up on *Aurora*'s deck with his camera and shot some photos of me rowing my boat. The pictures do indeed show a confident-looking rower, stroking purposefully even as her boat pitches wildly on frothing waves, the flag of the red ensign whipping horizontally in the strong breeze. In some of the shots nearly half of *Sedna*'s underside is visible as she rears out of the water. In other pictures she looks almost as if she is sinking, the large waves threatening to engulf her. But through it all I row on regardless. OK, I admit it—I knew there was a camera pointing at me and I was trying to impress.

After about fifteen minutes the crew of the *Aurora* bade me farewell and departed. It was a relief. Their visit had dented my fragile equilibrium. It had been strange to have a vessel alongside after getting so used to having the ocean to myself. For a couple of days afterward I could feel the phantom of the yacht lingering on, and it took me a while to shake the feeling that there was an object there that I needed to avoid. As time went by, I was becoming more comfortable in my solitude, and less inclined to want human contact.

A friend emailed me a question: "Are you lonely? Or has it kicked into being wonderful yet? And when you get a text, do you stop rowing to read it immediately (desperate for contact) or do you wait until your next break?"

Before I could answer the question I had to think hard about what she meant by loneliness. I decided that if it was a yearning for the company of a kindred spirit, then I had occasionally felt more lonely in a crowded room than I had ever been on the ocean. The daily conversations with my mother and the text messages that I would usually pick up two or three times a day seemed to be more than enough human interaction for me. I looked forward to those times, but I was not desperate for them. I was quite content with my own thoughts for company. Although I was keenly aware of the huge number of miles that separated me from dry land, and often felt intensely alone, I did not feel "lonely."

Loneliness had not been one of my demons. No, the demons that had plagued my first month on the ocean were feelings of inadequacy, self-doubt, and frustration. How could I not have realized this was going to be so hard? What had made me think I was up to it? Why was I not going faster? Why was it so hard to settle into a steady routine? The negative voices of Mr. Self-Doubt and Mr. Self-Critical had dominated my internal dialogue.

But since my epiphany about the discomfort zone being where I needed to be in order to grow, those negative voices had started to subside. My thoughts, which early on had been the cause of my mental malaise, were gradually becoming more constructive. Initially they had been responsible for plunging me into an abyss of negativity, but now they were carving the footholds and handholds to help me climb out from that abyss. I was learning to be kinder to myself.

I'd surprised myself with my ability to cope with practical problems, and was now giving myself due credit for my achievements. In other ways I'd disappointed myself—such as finding I was unable to endure sixteen hours of rowing a day—but with time I had accepted that these were my limitations, and had forgiven myself for them. And at last I seemed to be adapting to my new lifestyle. I no longer asked myself at the start of every rowing shift whether I wanted to do it, or could do it. I just went on and did it.

I had also found that doing something practical had the power to cheer me up. It gave me a sense of purpose, and temporarily quieted those negative voices in my head that sometimes threatened to overwhelm me. Tidying up the boat, or doing some basic maintenance, or writing a dispatch—all these things could distract me pleasantly for a while, and almost anything was a welcome break from the grinding monotony of rowing. Posting dispatches to my website was especially effective, as it allowed me to view my plight from one step removed, as if I were a character in a movie rather than a real person marooned in the middle of the ocean with very negative emotions. The attempt to find something interesting to write for the website forced me to be more upbeat and view my day more objectively, evaluating it objectively rather than emotionally.

Recently I had started thinking about an after-dinner speech I was due to give in New York the following April, planning what I would say I had learned from this experience. That exercise had helped me to see the present moment in the context of my whole life, and to put it in perspective. This process had been further aided by a couple of messages I'd received from friends. Among my most valued correspondents were a couple of other solo adventurers: Leven Brown, who was rowing the Columbus route from Cadiz to Jamaica, and Adrian Flanagan, who was sailing around the world via the Arctic and Antarctic. Around Christmas both of them, on the same day, had sent me words of advice that complemented each other. I flicked through my logbook to find the page where I had copied down their words, and their wisdom spoke to me across the expanses of ocean that separated us.

Leven: "Remember when the going is tough to treat it like a bad dream and focus on the welcome you are going to get in Antigua."

Adrian: "When you come to look back on it, the voyage will seem to have been over very quickly. Remember, it doesn't have to be fun to be fun. And it will have been fun once you are among the elite few who have single-handedly rowed an ocean."

Their words had helped me see that although right now I might prefer to be anywhere else, this time would pass, and it would be a lot more enjoyable in retrospect than it was right now. I had a great time preparing for the row, I would have a great time afterward basking in the glow of achievement, and if the bit in the middle was often hard going and sometimes rather miserable, that wasn't such a bad deal. No matter how unpleasant it was, it still had to be better than the bad old days when I worked in an office. It comforted me that although it seemed I had been on the ocean forever and would be forevermore, time and miles were passing, albeit slowly, and this episode of my life would eventually become a part of my past rather than a never-ending present.

As I rowed I had started to entertain myself with happy daydreams of life after rowing, picturing myself sitting at a dinner table surrounded by friends, tucking into fresh food, regaling the company with tales of the sea. I would entertain them with salty old stories, enlighten them with pearls of wisdom formed on the hard grit of experience, and inspire them with my shining example of fortitude and stoicism. If I could just stay true to my dream, it would all be worthwhile in the end.

To my relief, I finally found a new discipline in my rowing. When I had sat down to do that obituary exercise several years ago, it had brought home to me that if I carried on as I was, my future was not going to be what I wanted it to be. If I repeated what I did today 365 times, in a year's time I would not be any closer to where I wanted to be. My future was the accumulation of my todays—it was only by doing the right things, day after day, that I would create the future that I wanted. Just the same, if I wanted to get to Antigua, and soon, I had to make every day count.

At last I felt that I was getting into the swing of ocean rowing, and the ghastly, miserable first month was starting to seem like a fast-fading nightmare. Still, it was a fragile joy—I couldn't yet take the elation for granted, and I needed to nurture it carefully. There was still a long way to go, and possibly more trials in store for me. But I was starting to feel better equipped to deal with them than I had at the start.

fourteen

ATLANTIC HARDCORE

*t*he year 2006 arrived to find me still many miles from Antigua. After thirty-one days of rowing I had covered 665 miles, and still had 2,271 to go. I wasn't even a quarter of the way across.

But others were about to have an even worse time. Life for some of the competitors in the Atlantic Rowing Race was about to change from merely frustrating to positively life-endangering; 2006 was about to provide ample evidence that the ocean can be a dangerous place.

"Won't you be scared, being out there alone on the Atlantic?" people had asked me before the race. "It's dangerous."

"Life is dangerous," I had replied. "People in London can get on the commuter train one morning and be blown up by a terrorist bomb or maimed in a train crash. At least I'm on my guard against the danger—I've done everything I can to mitigate the risks."

Even if I had been quoted only a 90 percent chance of survival—which are good but not excellent odds—I would still have done it. Safety and security were no longer top priorities at this stage of my life. I had seen from the experience of others that a large bank balance didn't provide insurance against unhappiness, and wrapping myself in cotton wool was no guarantee against injury. It was better to get out there and live life, and to live it large, than to continue in my supposedly "secure" lifestyle, quietly dying of boredom.

I am not a brave person. I am not physically courageous in the way of daredevils who hurl themselves down black-diamond ski runs after their first two skiing lessons, or bounce their mountain bikes down narrow stony paths inches from a sheer cliff. I am very aware of the certainty of death, and am keen to delay it until the last possible moment. The truth is that I genuinely believed that I would survive the Atlantic. If I had thought for a moment that I was at serious risk of dying, I wouldn't have gone. But 2006 was to be an exceptional year. For the first time ever, the race organizers feared that they might have to break bad news to the next of kin.

Sunday, January 8, was when the trouble started, although the day had started well. At 1537 Greenwich Mean Time (1137 local time) *All Relative*, a men's four made up of two brothers and two cousins, became the first boat to cross the finish line in Antigua. Less than an hour later the celebrations were cut short when race HQ received the news of the first serious mishap of the race. *Digicel Atlantic Challenge*, manned by Gearoid Towey and Ciaran Lewis from Ireland, had capsized and failed to self-right. It appeared that the entire transom (the flat vertical panel that comprises the stern of the boat) had come off, flooding the aft cabin. The *Digicel* crew were picked up from their life raft by an eastbound container ship called the *Hispania Spirit*. In a strange twist of fate, two weeks later on its return leg westward, the same *Hispania Spirit* would rescue the two Pearson brothers from the life raft after their rowboat, too, had capsized.

Also on January 8, one of the crew members of *Gurkha Spirit* was thrown off their boat when it broached. He managed to get back on board, but sustained injuries to his ankle and his chest in the incident. On the same day, one of the four women on board the *Rowgirls Shelterbox* boat decided that her back pain was too severe for her to continue in the race, and requested the support yacht to come and collect her.

Only hours after the *Aurora* had collected the Rowgirl, they were called to assist the *Sun Latte* crew, who were under attack from a very aggressive twelve-foot shark. The shark had started buffeting the hull of their boat, and the crew were understandably terrified. On the advice of the support crew they withdrew to the cabin where they sat silent and motionless, hoping that the six millimeters (a quarter inch) of marine ply that separated them from their pelagic tormentor could withstand the onslaught. The crew survived the experience, but a few weeks later their hull started leaking, "most likely" as a result of the shark attack. When their boat then capsized, injuring one of the crew members, they decided they had had enough and withdrew from the race.

Less than a week after the shark attack, on January 15, the two-girl crew of *American Fire* suffered a capsize and spent surely the longest night of their lives clinging to the upturned hull of their boat while they waited for rescue. At last, sixteen hours later, an old-fashioned sailing ship in full rig hove into view. This was the *Stavros S. Niarchos*, a ship of the Tall Ships Trust that by pure coincidence I had toured in Portsmouth just before leaving Britain for the Canaries. It must have appeared to Emily and Sarah like a mirage when this magnificent ship appeared on the horizon, like a scene from *Pirates of the Caribbean*.

Another casualty was *Moveahead*, crewed by a pair of older men who had been moving at a relatively sedate pace near the back of the field. After they had overtaken me on my birthday I had fought back. For days now I'd had them figuratively in my sights and had been putting in an extra effort in a bid to overtake them, so determined was I not to come in last in the race.

After days of edging up to them only to fall back again when the weather turned in their favor, I finally overtook them. A few days later, on January 17, their boat sank, and I was back in last place again.

The last of the casualties was the *Spirit of Cornwall,* on January 22. It capsized when it was agonizingly near to Antigua. Just 180 miles separated them from the finish line when they suffered an unrecoverable capsize and had to abandon their attempt.

A number of the capsizing casualties had made the same mistake—they had left their cabin hatches open to allow fresh air to circulate. The cabins were the boats' buoyancy chambers: while they were sealed shut, the air trapped inside would ensure that the boat would come the right way up again if it capsized. If the hatch was open, the buoyancy chamber would be compromised: water would rush in, weighing more than the air it displaced, and the boat would stubbornly stay upside down. A day might appear calm, but it would take only one big wave to knock the boat down. As soon as water started gushing into the cabin their bid to row the Atlantic would be over. For a while we were bombarded with daily texts from Woodvale, urging us to keep our hatches shut at all times. I had always been careful in this regard, but now I became obsessive, peering out of the round hatch before I opened it to see if any large waves were about to strike, and slamming the hatch shut behind me as quickly as I could.

Most of the bad news left me sad for the afflicted, but otherwise unshaken. The exception to this was when my mother informed me in early January that Chris Martin, the other solo entry, had suffered a capsize and his boat had failed to self-right. Mum told me that the reason for his capsize was that he had been forced to drink his ballast water when his watermaker failed, and had then neglected to refill the ballast chambers with salt water. This meant that his boat was not as bottom-heavy as it should have been and this affected its ability to come the right way up after a capsize. It had only been with the greatest difficulty that he had managed to salvage the situation, by hanging on to the rudder and using his body weight plus the momentum of the waves to turn it the right way up again. He had lost his last two unbroken oars when the boat rolled, and had to sit and wait for several days until the support yacht could bring him replacements.

This conversation left me subdued and scared because Chris was the only other solo entry, so besides the fact that we'd had a few beers together back in London, I identified much more with him than with the other crews. When I hung up the phone I looked out of my round cabin hatch into the cockpit. Still fresh in my mind was a vivid image of Chris hanging on to his boat's rudder, desperately struggling to pull the boat right side up while waves crashed around him. The rowing seat waited expectantly for me to start my next shift, but today the prospect was even less appealing than usual. I regarded the waves with a new sense of awe, fear, and trepidation, and a fresh appreciation of just what they could do to me.

It was strange that fear came to me most vividly when there was no immediate reason to be afraid. Chris's mishap had happened hundreds of miles away, in a different weather system, in a different style of boat, and very different circumstances. There was no logical reason for me to be any more afraid at this moment than at any other. But fear is rarely logical.

Nor does fear have any reality—it exists only in the mind. You can't see a fear. I knew this, but there and then, sitting in my cabin with Mum's news still echoing in my mind and every fiber of my being resisting the idea of going out into that hostile environment, my fear seemed very real. I had to give myself a stern talking-to before I could muster the courage to go out and face the elements once more.

Apart from the initial fearful period of my voyage, when I lay quaking in my bunk, convinced that my rudder was going to snap off its pintles or that a container ship was going to run me over, this was the only time I felt really scared. There had been a few moments when I could have been terrified and with good reason, but seizing up in panic would have been a waste of precious time, and I was too busy doing what needed to be done in order to survive.

The closest I came to serious mishap was on January 14. The Atlantic started off in a playful mood—a gust of wind blew my baseball cap into the water. I lunged after it but the waves carried it away. I had a spare hat, but this one was my favorite. I had been using it since the start of the race so I had developed a sentimental attachment to it. Its loss was a sad blow. But as I crouched there, leaning on the gunwale, staring forlornly after the hat and regretting my latest contribution to ocean pollution, I saw it coming back toward me. The waves were gently ushering it back toward the boat. They brought it back within reach and I plucked it quickly from the water before it sank forever.

A little later I discovered another trick that the ocean had played on me. Locker number 7 contained nothing that I needed on a regular basis so I had not opened it for a while. Today I was looking for my handheld bilge pump, and when I lifted the locker lid soon after the baseball cap incident I found that it had flooded. The life jacket had self-inflated, as it was supposed to do when submerged. It would be inconvenient having to dry it out and repack it, but I supposed this was reassuring—at least it worked as it was supposed to. Worse news was that one of my drybags hadn't lived up to its description. This was my ditch bag, and held the vital items that I would need with me in the life raft if I abandoned ship. Miraculously the handheld GPS seemed to have survived its bath. I wasn't sure if my emergency rations of chocolate bars might react badly to being soaked in seawater, so I decided this was a good enough excuse to eat them immediately.

The electrical cables to the watermaker ran through locker 7, which caused me a moment's panic. I ran the watermaker and it still seemed to be working fine so I breathed a sigh of relief. Unfortunately the water had traveled through the gland where the wires penetrated the bulkhead, so had also flooded locker 5 which was on the other side of the bulkhead, underneath the floor of my cabin. This locker was relatively inaccessible so I had not put much in there—only my precious supply of clean, dry socks, which were a real treat at the end of a chilly night shift. I would pull them on before I climbed into my damp, salty sleeping bag, briefly enjoying the warm comfort of toasty toes. But now every last pair was soaked in seawater, and yet another creature comfort—along with hot food and a dry bed—was gone.

These concerns, though, were minor compared with what came later. That afternoon the mood turned nasty. I was emptying the bedpan over the side of the boat (the downwind side of the boat—I had learned the hard way that it was a bad idea to empty the pan upwind) when the boat had turned sideways to the waves, as it always did when I stopped rowing. I didn't even see the huge wave coming toward me from the other side of the boat. All I knew was that one moment I was dealing with my ablutions, and the next moment I was in the water—still on board, but the boat had tipped over so far that I was dunked headfirst into the briny sea. Everything turned blue and watery, as it had in my childhood dreams of drowning, and I screwed up my eyes and held my breath and wondered what was going to happen next. For what seemed like an eternity I clung on for dear life—to the guardrail oar with one hand, and my bedpan with the other—until at last *Sedna* turned herself right side up and I once again felt fresh air on my face. I opened my eyes to see the deck of the boat completely swamped. Various objects had escaped from the boat and were bobbing around in the waves nearby. I conducted a split-second stock-taking and decided what needed to take priority. My lunch, which I had put to rehydrate in a thermos mug in the mug holder, was bobbing off across the waves. My last beef chili casserole—my favorite! The sea anchor was also overboard, and rapidly self-deploying. I didn't have all its lines attached to the boat, and I couldn't afford to lose that. Lunch would have to wait. I quickly hauled the sea anchor back on board. My mug of chili casserole bobbed temptingly close, but just beyond arm's reach. I hung out over the side of the boat, straining to get to it, but the waves took it away from me. I watched sadly as it drifted out of view and was lost to the ocean.

I shuddered when I thought of what could have happened, and rowed on in a chastened mood for some time before recovering my spirits. I had not been clipped onto the boat at the time of the incident, and could easily have been washed overboard. If I had lost contact with the boat's guardrail, it could have been the end of me. If my boat and I had parted company I couldn't count on being as fortunate as my baseball cap, and solo rowers don't get second chances. As the wind speed approached thirty knots I clipped on and kept my eyes wide open for oncoming watery juggernauts.

Despite my recent scare I still managed to find something to smile about. It is odd the things that the mind chooses to focus on in a crisis. Any lingering fear that I could justifiably have felt was overshadowed by grief at the loss of my last portion of chili beef casserole.

fifteen

BETWEEN THE DEVIL
AND THE DEEP BLUE SEA

January dragged on, and my mother watched my little purple blob on the Woodvale chart make slow progress westward. Sid the sea anchor stayed on board as the winds remained in the east, and my average improved to about thirty miles a day. On January 27 I crossed the halfway point. It had taken me nearly two months to get this far. I wanted to believe Tiny when he told me that the second half would be quicker than the first. The prospect of four months at sea was more than I could bear.

But the conditions were not helpful. Although an ocean row-boat has limited capacity to respond to weather conditions, there were still tactical decisions to be made and every day I was presented with the decision of which way to point my bow. I was not completely at the mercy of the elements, and did not always have to go straight downwind. If the wind was gusting fiercely, my capacity for determining my own direction was minimal—I had to keep *Sedna* perpendicular to the waves, otherwise the boat would rapidly turn fully sideways-on, a broach position in which it was impossible to row. But if the gusts were not too strong, I could make progress at an angle of up to thirty degrees to the prevailing wind direction, using my rudder to keep me pointing diagonally across the waves. And if I was becalmed, I could go in almost any direction I chose, but very, very slowly.

I wished I'd had time to gain a better understanding of meteorology and oceanography, as I now had plenty of information but wasn't sure what to do with it. The Atlantic seemed to be full of potential hazards, and I found it confusing to weigh up all the competing factors of weather, wind, swell, and currents, and determine my best course of action.

On February 4, Tiny tipped me off that there was an eddy waiting to ambush me—a one-hundred-mile-diameter clockwise current, like a gigantic whirlpool, centered on 16.8°N 44.8°W. Tiny had been the victim of a hostile eddy during his own row. As he was approaching Antigua it had swept him fifty miles north and he had had to be towed to the island or else risk missing it altogether.

Tiny's news presented me with a dilemma: whether to head south to get the favorable current south of its center, but then risk problems getting north again to Antigua, or carry on at the same latitude and face a hard slog against the current. The word from Tiny was to head south. So I diverted to the southwest, in the hope that the eddy would slingshot me out the other side in the general direction of Antigua.

But later that same day I got an email from Ricardo, my new weatherman, which made the situation more complicated. Ricardo had been routing my sailing friend Adrian Flanagan and had now agreed to help me. He advised me that there was a massive low in the far North Atlantic that would bring a huge northwest swell— waves between seven and fifteen feet high. This swell would reach me by the following Monday, and would be strong enough to stop me in my westerly tracks. According to Ricardo, my best strategy would be to head northwest immediately to gain as much latitude as possible before the swell struck.

In summary, Monday looked like this: a swell pushing me southeast, the wind pushing me southwest, an eddy pushing me northwest, and I just wanted to go west.

The ocean was looking increasingly like an obstacle course, and I felt like Odysseus, stuck between Scylla and Charybdis. A bad decision now could add days to my journey, a journey that would already be plenty long enough. A dark cloud of uncertainty hung over *Sedna*.

Black Monday, as I had come to think of it, arrived. With the conflicting influences of the eddy, the wind, and the swell, the waves were coming at me from all directions and the going was heavy—less like rowing, and more like weightlifting. I usually rated about twenty strokes per minute, but that day the rating dropped to sixteen, and my usual speed of around two knots declined to a disheartening one knot.

Worse still, I broke an oar—again. It was not really surprising in these rough conditions. An oar that I had already repaired once had now bent and splintered in a different place. A sideswiping wave broke it just below the collar. I had done so many repairs by now that the process had become routine: out with the hacksaw and duct tape. Take the sacrificial oar—one oar was so far beyond repair that I was chopping it up and using sections of it to reinforce the repairs I made to the other oars—and saw a length off it. Take this splint and cut it along its length, wrap it around the breakage like a sleeve, and bind it up tightly with duct tape.

I regarded the repair with satisfaction, but my complacency was premature. A few hours later, another big wave came and the oar cracked again. Visions of waiting a week for a support yacht to bring replacements flashed across my mind's eye. I rejected the notion. I wasn't ready to give up my unsupported status just yet.

But what could I use for a splint? It seemed that the load on this breakage was too much for the splint made from the sacrificial oar. I needed something stronger. Both sections of the boathook were already in service, and I needed something straight, rigid, and at least a foot long. There was an option I'd considered previously—the axles from my spare rowing seat—but I hadn't been able to figure out how to dismantle it. I looked at it again, but even after calling boatbuilder Richard Uttley for advice I still couldn't get the bolts to shift. They seemed to have rusted into place. I would have to cut them free. So out came the hacksaw again, and after half an hour of strenuous sawing I had my splints.

This repair had used up the last of my duct tape. I had started out with three large rolls of it, but the frequent oar repairs had required every last inch, and I still had many miles to go. I wasn't sure what would come to an end first: my Atlantic row, my mending materials, or my limited supplies of toilet paper. Or, indeed, my patience.

sixteen

TWO HUNDRED VALENTINES

*i*t was a bright and breezy day in mid-February, with rapidly pass-ing squalls turning the sky from clearest blue to darkest black in a matter of moments. When the sun shone the sea was dazzling, the sunbeams reflecting off the water in a million bright sparkles. Then the fast-moving clouds would block the sun's rays and turn the water from sparkling silver to a seething darkness, the foamy white horses a stark contrast to the black waters beneath. The temperature fluctuated with the weather, but it was generally mild and I was wearing just a T-shirt, and a baseball cap with a thin snood over it to stop the strong wind blowing it off my head. The wind direction and the swell were favorable, and I was making good progress.

I had already been at the oars several hours when I heard the beep of a text arriving on my satellite phone. The message was from my mother:

HMS SOUTHAMPTON IMMINENT.

During the preparations for my row I'd had several contacts with the Royal Navy, who had been very supportive of my ven-ture. Although they were undergoing a period of major cutbacks and could offer little more than moral support, I had welcomed the association, feeling that it lent me credibility as a professional adventurer. I had gladly placed a large Royal Navy sticker on the roof of my bow cabin. The navy had tentatively offered to arrange a midocean rendezvous if they happened to have a ship in my part of the ocean while I was out there. I had all but forgotten about the offer, and although it had been nearly two months since I last saw a human face, the news provoked mixed feelings. Refreshing though it might be to have some face-to-face contact, I was worried about the effect it might have on my fragile discipline.

Once I had made myself decent for the visit—adding Lycra shorts to my outfit—I focused on getting myself mentally ready. I needed to keep a check on my emotions, to create a protective barrier around my core so that I could greet the HMS *Southampton* with all appropriate enthusiasm, but then after the visit be able to return to the oars and get on with business as usual. I hoped I could do it.

The morning wore on. I periodically looked over my shoulder to try to spot the ship, but there was no sign. I started to wonder what Mum had meant by "imminent." In this strange, slow-moving ocean world I was living in, imminent could mean anything from a few minutes to a couple of days.

I'd almost given up on my expected visitors when I glanced over my shoulder and saw a huge gray warship less than half a mile away. After so many days of seeing nothing but sea and sky and my own tiny boat, it was extraordinary to see this apparition, like a floating city, the sheer sides of its hull looming up like cliffs out of the water. Its superstructure was a complex hodgepodge of decks, walkways, hangars, and cabins. It bristled with satellite domes, radar dishes, and communications masts. A helicopter rested on its aft deck, looking like a toy in relation to the overall size of the ship.

It was an impressive sight, but I felt no buzz of adrenaline. Maybe my emotional self-protection was working. I leaned into the cabin and picked up the VHF radio handset.

"This is *Sedna Solo, Sedna Solo, Sedna Solo.* Come in, HMS *Southampton.*"

"This is HMS *Southampton*," a well-mannered English voice came back over the airwaves. It was strange to hear a male voice—for so long the only voices I had heard had been mine and my mother's. "We're glad to hear from you. We've been looking for you for hours."

I could understand the support yacht *Aurora* having difficulty in finding me, but I might have hoped that the Royal Navy, with the help of the advanced radar equipment evidenced by the forest of domes, dishes, and antennae, could be able to see me. It made me realize just how invisible I was—*Stealth Sedna.*

"We'd like to launch an inflatable boat to come over for an in-person rendezvous with you, but we're not sure if we can," the voice went on. "It's a bit rough out there."

I lurched to one side as a large wave broadsided my boat. "No kidding," I said.

I put away the handset and watched as a gray inflatable boat, tiny in comparison with its mother ship, appeared over the guardrail and was lowered to the water. It came bouncing across the waves toward me, the white ensign of the Royal Navy fluttering from the back of the boat, and four tiny figures gradually resolved themselves into real people as the craft approached. They were well clad against the elements, wearing yellow oilskins, life jackets, and helmets. A friend of mine would later comment, when she saw the photos of the encounter, that in my T-shirt and skimpy shorts either I was seriously underdressed for the conditions or they were seriously overdressed.

"Good morning!" they hailed me as they came alongside. "Happy Valentine's Day!"

Wow, so it was. I'd forgotten all about it, romance being the last thing on my mind in present circumstances. "And Happy Valentine's Day to you, too," I replied. "Good to see you."

This last was a tactful white lie. These men had gone to a lot of trouble to find me and no doubt imagined that they would be a welcome sight to this poor, lonely woman who would by now be desperate for human interaction, so it didn't seem appropriate to say that I was carefully preserving my indifference to the situation and was actually quite impatient to get back to the oars to make the most of the conditions, which were favorable for a good day's mileage.

"Where are you bound for?" I asked, shouting over the roar of the wind and the waves. I wasn't used to making mid-Atlantic small talk, but this seemed like an appropriately seafaring question to ask. The man at the wheel was struggling to keep their craft alongside while not colliding with *Sedna*, the rough seas making it hard to control the bucking boat.

"We're on our way from Grenada back to the U.K.," came the reply.

"Go on, make me jealous, tell me how long it's going to take you to get there."

"Probably ten to fourteen days, depending on the weather. Our top speed is thirty knots."

I thought ruefully of the two and a half months I had already spent on the ocean, and the many more days still to go before I reached my destination. In cruel contrast with their top speed of thirty knots, my personal best was four knots and my average was about two.

"We've got something for you." One of the men waved a black plastic bag.

"I don't know if I'm allowed to accept anything." I was alarmed. I was coming last in the race, but I had fought hard to maintain unsupported status, refusing to give in to pressure from emails and texts urging me to take mercy on my shoulders and call for replacement oars when the last two had broken. If I had accepted any kind of material assistance it would have constituted support and would, in my eyes, have utterly devalued the significance of my row as a declaration of independence. No matter how long it took me, I was determined to do it alone.

"It's OK, we checked it out with Woodvale and they said this was allowed. It's not food, it's a Valentine's card."

They maneuvered in closer to my boat, their rubber hull bouncing off *Sedna*'s side as they reached out to hand me the black bag. It didn't feel right reaching out to accept it, but I didn't want to appear ungrateful for their gallantry, so I took it. As I did an image flashed through my mind. I had heard a story about an ocean rower who, just as he was approaching his final destination, had been hailed by someone on a passing yacht who had thrown him a can of cola. Instinctively he had reached out to catch it. That can of cola had cost him his unsupported status. No matter what Woodvale had said, I wasn't happy about accepting this Valentine. But even in midocean, I felt that manners mattered and it would be rude to refuse it.

"Thank you very much," I said. "Sorry I don't have one for you. Slipped my mind."

I peeked inside the bag. There was just a single cream-colored envelope. No chocolates, no food, so maybe it was all right. A card didn't exactly constitute material assistance if I couldn't eat it, drink it, or row with it. Even so, I hid it furtively behind my back as the officers circled *Sedna* to snap some photos of me with HMS *Southampton*. I didn't want the bag to appear in the photographs.

"We would have brought you a bacon butty [sandwich], but that was definitely not allowed. And the captain said you'd be most welcome to come over to his quarters for a hot bath, but that's not allowed, either."

"Some new oars would be even more welcome, but that would definitely count as support."

We chatted for a bit longer and then they bade me calm seas and following winds, and with a farewell roar of their outboard

engine they headed back to the *Southampton* and their bacon butt-
ies and hot baths.

I watched them go, the inflatable launch lurching across the
rough seas, crashing down off the backside of waves. I felt relieved
to be alone again on my little boat. After so long alone it had been
a mild strain to make conversation with strangers, and the black
bag felt strange in my hand. It was the first foreign object to be
introduced to my world since I had left the Canaries. I had become
familiar with every single thing that I had on board, knew precisely
what I had and where to find it, and it felt weird to be holding
this unfamiliar item. I regarded it suspiciously, like an unwelcome
intruder. I opened the hatch and stuffed it into my cabin, and
returned to the oars and watched as the launch arrived back at the
ship and was winched up on davits to the deck.

Then the *Southampton* approached and steered alongside me,
Her Majesty's ship looking impressively huge as she loomed over
Sedna. She sounded her klaxon and my eardrums resounded with
the strange, man-made noise. The men on deck waved to me and
I waved back, then the great ship pointed herself east and with a
roar of her engines and a stench of diesel fumes she cruised off into
the distance.

It had been a very special Valentine, but maybe not for the reasons that the Royal Navy imagined. It was special for me because
my spell had worked. I had succeeded in protecting my kernel of
equanimity in the face of this potential disruption. The encounter
had been pleasant, but I was happy to be alone once again. It was
time to get rowing and make the most of this strong easterly wind
while it lasted. It was without any sense of loss that I watched the
Southampton fade to a speck and then disappear over the horizon,
leaving me to my watery world, a world in which at last I was
beginning to feel more at ease.

Later, as I finished the last three-hour shift, I reflected on my day. I was wearing just a T-shirt and a hat, and the tropical night air was velvety against my skin. The sun had set about two hours prior, and the afterglow had finally faded from the western sky, where a thin crescent moon was now hanging like a silver hammock. I could see its reflection dancing in the hatch door in front of my rowing position, and my moon shadow rowed diligently away before me. The Perspex dome of my compass nightlight was glowing red between my feet, but I preferred to steer by the stars, lining up Orion's belt with the pole of the gently fluttering red ensign.

It was a calm night, and the ocean was almost silent, a faint sighing its only sound. My oars, broken and repaired, each had its own distinctive splash. The left one, with spoon intact, made a clean entry into the water, while the right one, spoon lashed to a boathook with cable ties, made a messier splash, with the occasional gurgle as a bubble escaped from the hollow tube of the broken shaft.

It was at night, as I rowed along beneath the great glittering canopy of the stars, that I felt most aware of the hugeness of the ocean, and the smallness of myself. But it was not a scary or intimidating feeling—it was a feeling of wonder and amazement that I was here, more than a thousand miles from the nearest land, alone and rowing away in a little silver boat. My situation was so absurd and yet so magnificent.

The alarm on my watch went off to signal the end of my shift and I stowed my oars for the night, with a satisfying feeling of a job well done—another day and a few more miles closer to Antigua. I gazed up at the Milky Way while I brushed my teeth, idly wondering if in all those worlds orbiting all those stars there might possibly be another solitary woman looking up at the stars from an ocean rowboat. Then I retired to my cabin to write up my logbook and go to bed, where I would dream peaceful dreams of dry land, family, friends, and food.

seventeen

INCOMMUNICADO

*O*n February 17, my seventy-ninth day at sea, and seven hundred miles from Antigua, my satellite phone failed, thus severing my only means of communicating with anyone on dry land.

The phone had never been 100 percent reliable, but that was the nature of satellite communications. I was using the Iridium system, which depends on a network of low-orbiting satellites about five hundred miles above the earth's surface to relay the telephone signal. Each satellite circles the earth roughly once every hour and a half. In theory the coverage is complete and continuous, but in practice I had found that the signal strength would come and go as the satellites moved, dropping the call. This often seemed to happen when I was in the middle of a data transmission, sending text and photos to my website. If I lost the connection during such a call I would have to start over again, which at a cost of $1.50 per minute was irritating and expensive.

Voice calls, however, had seemed relatively reliable—until now. Occasionally I would call Mum and she wouldn't be able to hear me, so I would hang up and try again and it would usually work at the second attempt. It was unusual to lose a call in midconversation, but this was what happened that morning.

We had been having our usual daily check-in and Mum was telling me about the latest crews to arrive in Antigua. I was feeling almost unbearably envious of them for being there already, when suddenly the phone went dead. I looked at the small green-and-black screen on the handset. It was blank. The phone had turned itself off. I tried pressing the on button. The display lit up and the word *Searching* appeared while the handset tried to establish contact with the circling satellites. After a few seconds of searching the word disappeared and the handset turned itself off again. I was puzzled. This was not supposed to happen. Normally it would find a signal and the word *Iridium* would appear, along with two segmented bars, one showing the amount of power still in the battery, the other showing the strength of the satellite signal. The battery bar showed that the phone was fully charged, so that wasn't the problem. I jabbed at the on button a few more times, in the way that the technologically challenged do when they have no better ideas. Unsurprisingly, this had no effect.

I sat back and asked myself how I felt about this latest development.

Guilty delight. Relief at not having to set the alarm for the middle of the night to conduct radio interviews. Freedom from guys texting me to offer unsolicited advice or ask me out to dinner. Escape from the daily weather forecasts that had sent my mood skyrocketing or nosediving—and were usually wrong anyway. I relished the prospect of having peace and quiet at last, and the opportunity to truly test myself and find out if I had learned the lessons that the ocean had tried to teach me.

Until this point I hadn't realized the strength of the umbilical cord that still attached me to shore. I had thought I was alone because I had no physical contact, but I had still had plenty of human interaction. While I had the telephone I could still speak and be spoken to, I could send and receive texts, I could send dispatches to my website, I could even receive emails. Now I was totally alone. If I had to call for help I could press the red button on my EPIRB, the Emergency Position-Indicating Radio Beacon, while my Argos beacon would still beam back my position to race headquarters, but these were now my only means of communication with shore.

I like to believe that everything happens for a reason. For weeks now I had been asking myself, "Why am I still on this ocean? I've learned everything I can learn about myself. I'm bored and I'm tired and I want to go home. Why am I being kept out here for so long?" Now, to my way of thinking, the reason was clear. I had needed to stay out here this long to give my satellite phone time to fail. This was when life would start to get really interesting. For better or worse I was on my own now, and would have to manage without the moral support from my mother or anybody else.

Even before the race started I had mixed feelings about being in contact with others while I was on the ocean. I was almost envious of the sailors who voyaged the world in the days when nobody would know whether they were alive or dead until they arrived— or failed to arrive—at their destination. That seemed to me the purest, most courageous, most independent form of adventure— the ultimate test of self-reliance.

But the satellite phone had been a required piece of equipment for all competitors in the race, so I'd had no choice in the matter. It was indeed an important safety device; the EPIRB could raise an alarm, but did not allow the crew to state the problem or explain how serious it was. The emergency beacon was to be used only in situations of imminent danger, when death seemed a strong possibility. The satphone could be used in less serious situations, to request assistance or resupply. I could, of course, have refused to use the phone, but I regarded it as an important aspect of my mission that I should share the adventure with others who might not be in a position to have an adventure of their own, but could enjoy it vicariously through my blogs and updates.

But now that the choice had been taken away from me, I was delighted that I was going to have the opportunity for complete solitude and peace. In everyday life I often felt bombarded by visual and aural input—road signs, advertisements, shop windows, warnings, Walk, Don't Walk, car stereos, construction work, reversing trucks—and even on the ocean there had sometimes seemed to be too much going on, too much external input interfering with my ability to think clearly. Now, this latest breakage had stripped away one of the biggest distractions, and I had moved one step closer to the purity and tranquillity that I had been looking for.

Also, one of my objectives in wanting to spend time alone on the ocean had been to know who I was when I was alone—away from the hopes, expectations, perceptions, and projections of other people. I had grown up, as many women have, wanting to be liked, seeking approval, trying to live up to expectations. Starting from a very early age I had developed a persona, a public face that I presented to the world in order to gain acceptance. So I had learned to be interested in rugby and cricket, pretended to enjoy live comedy, tried to appreciate classical music, feigned a taste for vodka shots—all in order to fit in. By the time I was an adult, it was not easy to distinguish the public face from the real person behind it, the pretend likes from the real likes.

While I had been alone for a month in the cottage in Ireland a couple of years previously, I had begun to unearth the person that lay behind the façade. As the month had gone on, I started to experience a strange sensation whenever I caught sight of myself in the mirror, as if I were seeing someone who looked familiar but whom I hadn't seen in a long time, like a long lost friend. One of my objectives in being on the ocean was to once again get back to the core of what it meant to be me, beneath the veneer of social conditioning. But it had been harder to do this while I was still in touch with the world outside.

There had been many times that I had been tempted to throw the phone overboard, or at least turn it off for several days at a stretch, and only consideration for my mother had prevented me from doing so. Now it seemed that circumstances had presented me with the opportunity that I had wanted all along.

I may have been pleased at this latest development, but my glee was still mixed with guilt and concern for my mother. For her, I knew this would be torture. On a few previous occasions when I had not managed to establish a data connection via the satphone, but had still been able to place a voice call, she had posted a dispatch on my behalf. As I would later find out, she now did so again, and her words conveyed her anxiety.

Day 80: Waiting for News
18 Feb 2006
Written by Rita Savage

All day I have waited for the telephone to ring but Roz has not phoned. I have checked her progress on the Atlantic Rowing Race website times without number. Sedna Solo *is moving, though the mileage on Friday and today have not been as good as the previous few days. One good thing is that although the wind is east-northeast and would be moving the boat southwest,* Sedna *has moved a bit more to the north, toward latitude 17 where she needs to be to reach Antigua. This can only mean that Roz is working hard at clawing back the degrees south where the wind and waves had taken her. A good sign in more ways than one.*

I do hope and pray that whatever the problem is with the communications that it can be overcome.

Mum had no idea what was happening to me. She could only track the purple dot of the signal from my Argos beacon as it edged slowly across the chart on the Woodvale race website. She could see that the purple dot was moving, but she didn't know for sure that the beacon was still on my boat or, for that matter, if I was still on the boat. If I had been hit by a particularly brutal wave, or large ship, it would be entirely possible that boat, beacon, and lifeless body had become separated. Although my mother is a practical woman, and not much given to morbid fantasies, it must have been hard for her, in the dark hours of the night, to not fear the worst. It was still less than two years since we had lost my father, and the memories of bereavement were still fresh in my mother's mind. When my satellite phone expired, she would tell me later, she felt like she had been bereaved all over again.

Worst of all for Mum was that there was nothing she could do. When the going gets tough, my mother likes to get going. She needs to get active, to do something proactive and positive to reassert control over the situation. When my father died she had hurled herself energetically into clearing out his study, recycling his papers, giving away his books, and redecorating the room to eradicate the lingering reek of the cigarettes that she blamed for his death.

But in this present situation there was frustratingly little that she could do. There was no outlet for her anxious energy. All she could do was sit and wait. She spent sleepless nights wondering if there was some action that I would want her to take, whether she should ask Woodvale to send out a support yacht to check that I was all right. She tried to guess what I would want her to do, her thoughts reaching out to me across the miles of ocean, and concluded that I would prefer to be left alone.

She was right. I was happy in my solitude. But for Mum's sake I felt obliged to attempt, however halfheartedly, to fix the phone.

I had already established that it was not the battery. Maybe it was the antenna. The handset was connected via a detachable connection to a long, thick cable that ran through the cabin roof and inside the tube of the rollbar to an external aerial. I detached the indoor end of the antenna cable from the phone and wiped the contact on its end. I looked into the penny-sized hole on the back of the handset where the antenna connection went in, and wiped the contacts in there, too. I reconnected the antenna and tried again, but still the phone refused to work.

Somewhere in the back of my mind, a memory was stirring. This scenario seemed familiar. Had somebody else had a similar problem? I wracked my brains, trying to remember a conversation that had taken place several months ago in what now seemed like a different lifetime, back in the days when I was a land-dwelling creature and had face-to-face conversations with real people. Who might I have been discussing satphones with?

Slowly I dredged the memory out of the deep recesses of my mind. I had been talking with Peter Beardow, the avuncular satphone geek who runs 7E Communications. There wasn't much that Peter didn't know about satellite phones. He had been telling me about a problem that another ocean adventurer, Dominic Mee, had had with his phone. Dom had been attempting to sail a kite-propelled boat across the North Atlantic when his Iridium had started "shorting out" in the connection between the antenna and the handset. What did "shorting out" mean? Something to do with electricity—the electrical circuit completing itself via the wrong route so the power didn't get to where it was supposed to go. Was that it? I looked at the chunky Iridium handset in my hand. I couldn't see how to apply this information to it. The end of the antenna just plugged into the back of the handset—how and where could anything be short-circuiting?

More of the memory was coming back, a recollection of Peter

saying, "We suggested he use a chocolate wrapper to fix it, but then he got overtaken by events." The events in question were that Dom and his tiny craft were hit by a hurricane and capsized. After activating his emergency beacon to summon assistance, Dom had spent twenty-four hours clinging to the kite-boat in huge waves and fifty-five-knot winds before he was rescued. His broken sat-phone had been the least of his worries while he fought to stay alive.

A chocolate wrapper. What kind of chocolate wrapper? Foil, presumably, rather than paper, as something metallic seemed more applicable to electronics. I didn't have any foil chocolate wrapper, but I had some foil from the back of a pack of painkillers. I peeled off a piece.

But what was I supposed to do with it? I sat cross-legged in my cabin, handset in one hand, piece of foil in the other, looking from one to the other in bafflement. I simply didn't have enough information about how to do this, and even if I happened to hit upon the right way to use the foil, this solution had never been proven to work, since Dom had been interrupted by the storm. The task seemed hopeless, but I felt I should at least try. I tried putting the foil in various positions around the connection between the hand-set and the antenna. After each attempt I would turn the phone on again and try to get a connection, but I got the same result every time: "Searching," followed by shutdown.

Over the next few days I would keep trying to get a connection on the phone, thinking that maybe the problem was due to damp-ness inside the unit and once the phone had dried out it might start working again. But it didn't.

I had seven hundred miles to go. If all went well I would be in Antigua in about two weeks. It seemed like just about the right amount of time to achieve my final objective—to discover myself—and the perfect, dramatic finale to my adventure. I wouldn't have intentionally put myself in this situation, but it seemed to me that the script was perfect.

The morning after the satellite phone failed, I woke up with a feeling of eager anticipation. Everything felt different. I felt more alive, more alert than before. I looked around my watery world with fresh eyes. At last I was alone!

The day turned hot, and the wind died. Gentle waves lapped peacefully at the hull of my boat. My progress was slow without the wind to help me, so I concentrated on my rowing technique, aiming to maximize efficiency by making a good connection between oar and water. I started to recite little mantras in my head, coaching myself to row better. "With every stroke, a little bit closer, a little bit nearer, to Antigua." Another mantra was inspired by a phrase that Tiny Little had used in one of his last text messages to me, admiring my tenacity: "I'm tougher than most, I'm tougher than most."

Over the course of my voyage I had compiled a list on my whiteboard of flattering words that people had used in messages to me, admiring my *self-belief, resourcefulness, courage, determination, discipline, dedication, humor, resilience,* and *strength.* Initially my reaction to such compliments had been, "Who, me?" but as time had gone on I had started thinking, "Why not me?" and had started to deliberately cultivate the behaviors consistent with these positive attributes. Now I incorporated them into the affirmations that I repeated to spur myself on.

I also had a list of numbers on my whiteboard—a countdown of the last five hundred miles remaining between me and Antigua, in increments of five miles. As I reached each milestone I would cross the number off the list. Progress in these conditions was slow, but at least I could reassure myself that every mile rowed was one mile closer to the end.

I was living my life by numbers. Not only was I counting down the miles toward my destination, but I was also counting the hours in the day and the rowing strokes in the hour. It was a poor substitute for music or other entertainment, but at least it gave me something to focus on and helped keep the negative voices at bay. I was averaging about a thousand strokes an hour, or around twenty strokes a minute once I'd deducted the hourly ten-minute break. I would count up to five hundred, and then down again. There were certain numbers that I greeted like old friends, familiar landmarks among other, more ordinary numbers. My favorites were those that represented the points of the compass—90, 180, 270 and 360. I also liked 111, 222, 333, and 444. As I reached them I would feel a little thrill of recognition, and a small celebration at having rowed a few more strokes toward English Harbor. It was not exactly scintillating, but it helped to reassure me that time was passing.

As the day wore on it got hotter and hotter. The solar panels were working at full capacity, charging my batteries. I could afford to be extravagant with my electricity, especially now that most of my electrical devices had broken, so I ran the watermaker for as long as necessary to fill all four of the red plastic jerry cans, and then some extra to fill my last remaining bucket, all the others having vanished overboard at various times. The sun beat down harshly, reflecting off the pale deck and the silver-painted bulkheads, dazzling my eyes and making me feel light-headed, so every hour during my break I removed my sunhat to dip it in the bucket of cool, fresh water and slap it back on my head so the water cascaded down over my sweating body, providing welcome relief. At twelve o'clock I reached the end of a rowing shift and took a quick sponge bath to cool down in preparation for my noonday nap.

Every moment of rest was precious, so I had the sponge bath down to a finely honed routine that took less than five minutes. I unstrapped my feet from the footplate, then took off my shoes and tied them onto a grabrail so they couldn't get washed overboard if a rogue wave came along. Then I sat down with my feet in a bucket of water in the bottom of the footwell while I splashed water over myself with a sponge. I squeezed a dollop of my favorite shower gel—mint and tea tree—onto the sponge and lathered myself all over, standing up to do my lower body.

As I bathed I hummed David Bowie's "Space Oddity." The lyrics, about a spaceman who loses contact with Planet Earth, seemed especially appropriate today. I was still having shoulder trouble, and the effect of the painkillers combined with the dazing effect of the sun and the loss of communications to make the day seem strange and surreal, as if my powers of perception had been subtly enhanced by a mind-altering drug.

> For here am I sitting in a tin can far above the world.
> Planet Earth is blue and there's nothing I can do.

I reached over the side of the boat and rinsed the sponge in the sea to avoid making the water in the bucket too soapy. Then I used the sponge to squeeze water over myself, sluicing the suds away into the footwell, which I would pump out later. The cool water revived my sun-fried brain and the tangy scent of the shower gel made my skin tingle with pleasure.

I marveled at how different I felt now that I had no way of obtaining a weather forecast. There was nothing to raise my hopes of good progress or arouse fears of adverse conditions. I couldn't post a dispatch to my website, so there was nothing to plan while I rowed. There would be no beeps of the phone to let me know that a text message had arrived. There was just the present moment, and in that moment there was only me, my boat, and this big blue ocean. After all my deliberate efforts to accept what came with Zen-like equanimity, the loss of my communications had made it all so easy. At last I had found serenity.

I relished my newfound self-sufficiency. With the watermaker droning away, chickpeas growing in the seed sprouter, and plenty enough food to see me to Antigua, I looked around at my orderly boat and felt, possibly for the first time, utterly at ease in the ocean environment. I had experienced this same feeling when I was trekking in Peru, knowing I had my tent, sleeping bag, and enough food for a week stowed away in my rucksack. I remembered gazing into the campfire one starlit night and reveling in the feeling of having all I needed, not needing to rely on anyone else for anything. I had dreamed that a solo ocean row would provide an opportunity for physical self-sufficiency and emotional self-reliance. Now I had found that sweet spot, and felt powerfully energized by it.

The next day I recorded a few minutes of video diary, talking into my handheld camcorder. Usually I recorded this inside my cabin, as I hadn't been able to afford a waterproof housing for my video camera so I preferred to keep it indoors for safety. But on this particular day the conditions were calm enough for me to venture outdoors with the camera, and the footage shows me standing on the deck of my boat in bright sunshine. A few other things are different, too, that make this footage stand apart from the hours of video I had shot before. For once I am not wearing a hat. I have just washed my hair and the wind is toying with my loose blond locks. My skin looks slightly weatherbeaten, and the corner of my mouth is chapped, but otherwise I look radiantly healthy—and, for the first time, truly happy. This sets today apart from all the other days, when I have grumbled and griped and grimaced to the camera. Today I am smiling into the camera as I speak.

"It's the second day since my satellite phone stopped working, and I can hardly find the words to describe how different I feel. I'm loving it. I feel like I'm starting to regain my energy. I've been rowing along this afternoon, feeling so serene and calm. It's been one of those really magic moments. If I could just bottle this feeling"—I pause for a moment—"I'd make millions."

I look out across the ocean, which is sparkling in the background. I no longer regard it as my enemy, I regard it as my salvation. I continue: "This feeling is better than any drug—a feeling of total self-sufficiency, self-reliance—just me and my little boat in the middle of the ocean. I'm happy and content. I've never known peace like it. It's an absolute total . . . peace. Yeah, there's no other word for it. It's made it all worthwhile—all the agony, all the suffering, all the pain, all the self-doubt. It's all been worth it for the way I feel this afternoon."

The recording ends.

eighteen

SHIPS PASSING IN THE NIGHT

i was revelling in my newfound contentment, but three thousand miles away, on the other side of the Atlantic, my mother was wracked by anxiety. I knew that she would be worrying about me, and so I tried to think of a way that I could convey to her that I was all right. I thought about turning my Argos beacon on and off, in a kind of improvised Morse code, to show that the beacon and I were still together and on the boat. But I was worried that this may in fact cause more consternation than reassurance. What happened if for some reason the Argos beacon didn't manage to reestablish its satellite connection? The purple dot would disappear from the map on the Woodvale website and Mum would assume the worst.

I could press the red button on the EPIRB. This would send a message to the United Kingdom's international maritime rescue coordination center in Falmouth, England, where the EPIRB was registered, telling them that I was in trouble and needed assistance. But I wasn't in trouble, and assistance was the last thing I wanted. The beacon is intended for use only in situations of "grave and immediate danger," when rescue is urgently required, and no matter

how concerned Mum may be feeling, a faulty satphone hardly constituted a life-threatening emergency.

So my best option seemed to be to hail a passing ship on my
VHF radio. The only problem with this plan was that there were
no passing ships. The radio worked by line-of-sight, so the other
vessel would have to be within a few miles of my position, and I
hadn't seen any ships since the HMS *Southampton* on Valentine's
Day, and very few before that. As the days went by I would stand
up at the end of every shift and scan the horizon for vessels, but
there was nothing to be seen apart from waves and sky.

It was about twelve days after my satphone had stopped working, and I was halfway through the final shift of the day. The last
light of the sun had already faded from the western sky. Suddenly,
across the darkened sea, I noticed some navigation lights off to
my left. A ship! And a large one, too, judging from the distances
between the pinpricks of light.

I stowed my oars and climbed into the cabin to try to hail them
on the radio. I found out later that I had caused great consternation on the bridge of the USS *Pomeroy*. Martin Wedderien was the
officer on duty, and it was his responsibility to check the radar on a
regular basis. It was he who would later tell me his end of the story.

A burly, amiable man from Seattle, Martin had just completed
his checks and had established for a fact that there were no other
vessels in the area. Suddenly a small English female voice piped up
on the VHF radio: "This is *Sedna Solo, Sedna Solo, Sedna Solo,* calling the very large ship to the west of me. Over."

Martin stared at the radio in astonishment. This couldn't be.
The radio's range was limited to its line-of-sight, so if there was
a vessel close enough to be heard on the radio, it had to be close
enough to appear on his radar. But the radar screen showed no tell-
tale blips. He turned around to his female colleague suspiciously.
"Are you messing me around?" he asked.

She raised her eyebrows and held her hands up in an expression of innocence. "Not me," she said.

Martin slowly picked up the radio handset and spoke hesitantly. "*Sedna Solo*, this is USS *Pomeroy*. Over."

"Hi there. Am I glad to see you! I just wanted to make sure that you see me, so you don't run me over."

"What kind of vessel are you, *Sedna Solo*?"

"I'm an ocean rowboat, twenty-four-foot long. I set out from the Canaries last November. I'm bound for Antigua."

"You're a rowboat? You've rowed from the Canaries?"

"Er, yup."

"Okayyyy . . ."

"And I wonder if you might be able to get a message to my mother. Do you have a satellite phone? Mine has stopped working."

"Sure. We've got everything—satphone, email—all the state-of-the-art communications stuff you could wish for."

"Great. Let me give you her phone number and email address . . ."

Day 93: Like a Ship Passing in the Night
3rd March
Written by Rita Savage

Great excitement today! This morning there was an email from a commercial ship: "Hey all, 2300Z (or thereabouts) March 2. I just passed Roz in position 17–01.145N X 058–05.393W. She sounds good, says she needs nothing and would appreciate it very much if I wouldn't run her over with my 950 ft long ship. She asked a very understandable question as our conversation developed . . . 'Do I sound sane to you, Martin?' . . . Ha! I couldn't bring myself to say . . . 'Well Roz, you did leave the Canary Islands in a rowboat three months ago,' so I said . . . 'Sure!!' Roz, it was a pleasure to talk to you.—Martin" (Martin L. Wedderien, Second Officer on USS Pomeroy)

There followed an exchange of emails as I inquired if there was any further crumb of information after two weeks of silence. One reply confirmed that the problem was indeed satphone failure. There was also a phone call direct from the ship, so Roz had obviously given them my telephone number in spite of the fact that she thought I might already be in Antigua. Thanks guys!

Further exciting news is that she is back above latitude 17 degrees and the wind is east-southeast, blowing her slightly north instead of south, for a change. Roz will probably have less than two hundred miles to go by the time you read this message.

nineteen

ONE HUNDRED DAYS OF SOLITUDE

*i*t was March 2, and two weeks had now passed since the demise of my satellite phone. I was sure that all the other crews must have finished, and if I had been in contact with the real world I might have been smarting at being the last one left out on the ocean. But since my satellite phone had stopped working the real world had receded to a distant memory, and the opinions of people there mattered to me not at all. When I had been speaking with my mother every day, reality had seemed closer at hand. I would picture her sitting in her study, holding the phone to her ear, tapping away on her computer keyboard while she looked up the positions of the other crews in the race, or consulting her notes to remind herself of the things she needed to say to me. Back then I had minded more that I was the straggler at the back of the pack.

Now I no longer had that daily check-in with the real world—a world where people slept in proper beds, lived in houses, drove cars, went to work, and spent time with friends—and I had almost forgotten that it existed. My world was here, on an increasingly stripped-down and rust-stained boat, surrounded by blue ocean and blue sky. This was my reality now, and felt as if it had always been so.

My whole raison d'être had become my safe arrival in Antigua. I rarely thought of anything else. I had no dispatches to prepare and no incoming questions or comments to stimulate fresh lines of thought. I was becoming a rowing automaton, repeating my mantras and telling myself that I was going to make it—just keep going, just keep rowing.

But I could not totally tune out. There still remained the tricky issue of trying to hit Antigua. In the vast expanse of the Atlantic, Antigua was a tiny dot on the chart. It was like trying to land a parachute onto a penny. During a pre-race briefing meeting with Woodvale, Lin Barker had given us some advice about navigation: "You're not in sailing boats. You're not going to be able to steer all that accurately. So don't worry too much about your course for the first couple of thousand miles. Just aim west and a bit south. Then when you're in the last few hundred miles you can start thinking about how you're going to get to Antigua."

She had gone on to say that in the previous year's race, at one point the northernmost crew had been five hundred miles north of the southernmost crew. From what my mother had told me it seemed that this year's race had been no different, with the colored blobs representing the twenty-six crews meandering erratically across the map of the Atlantic like a bizarre marine version of Wacky Races.

I had heard that some of the crews had found it difficult to cross the official finish line, an imaginary line extending out to sea for one mile from the Cape Shirley lighthouse on the south coast of Antigua. Some crews had been swept too far south, toward the rocky coast of Guadeloupe, while others had been blown north. One women's pair had been in danger of being swept straight past Antigua and had accepted a tow into Seatons, a harbor on the north coast. If crews of two had been struggling to make landfall in the right place, I knew that it would be a miracle if I, rowing solo in a lightweight boat with considerable wind resistance, managed to hit the target of the one-mile-long finish line.

At one point, a few weeks previously, the wind had seemed quite determined that instead of going to Antigua I would be going south to Barbados instead. For a while I was quite amenable to the idea—at that point I was just eager to see any dry land. I had even texted the race organizers to say that I might aim for this alternative destination. They had texted back that this would be a shame, as "The whole of Antigua is waiting for you," and this promise of a warm welcome, combined with a shift in the wind, had re-established Antigua as my intended destination.

I knew where I wanted to go. And my GPS told me where I was. But connecting the two was another matter altogether. The wind was making life very difficult for me, as were the occasional eddies that lay in wait. I had intended to reach the line of latitude of Antigua—seventeen degrees north—and follow this notional line straight to the finish, but the wind seemed to have other ideas. As soon as I got even a half-mile north of the line, the wind swept me north. If I strayed to the south, the wind swept me yet farther south. Maintaining a course along the seventeenth parallel seemed like balancing on a tightrope—and it was very easy to fall off.

As I approached the last two hundred miles of the race, the conditions became increasingly fickle, and my navigational anxieties grew. I would look at my chartplotter and check on the two lines extending from the blinking dot that represented my present position. One line led straight from me to the final waypoint: the Cape Shirley lighthouse. The other line represented my present course. The chartplotter display was inside my cabin, so naturally whenever I was looking at it I was not rowing and the second line therefore showed my angle of drift, rather than the angle I was steering while I rowed. This drift was the product of wind, swell, and current. When I had been becalmed and my drift was nonexistent, this line would wheel wildly around the chart, my momentum so slight that the instrument didn't know where to point. Now the drift was more purposeful-looking, but not in the right direction. It was always too far north or too far south. I became obsessed with it, swearing at the screen and willing the line to point the way I wanted it to. While I was rowing I would pray for the wind to shift and stare fixedly at my red ensign flag, which had become my makeshift wind indicator since my anemometer had seized up with rust a couple of months previously. Sometimes the breeze would give a couple of teasing gusts, raising my hopes, only to shift back again to its previous unhelpful bearing.

On the second day of March, my state of mind was fairly neutral. I had made poor mileage overnight—I remembered with faint envy that Tiny had told me that on a good night he had done more than twenty miles; my best so far was a paltry eleven—but I had now come to accept that prodigious overnight mileages were just not my fate this time around. Yet I was still optimistic that I could complete my crossing in under one hundred days. I had just under two hundred miles to go, and eight days to do them. I would need to average twenty-five miles a day, and my average daily mileage in February had been thirty-six and a half miles, so my optimism was well-founded. I was certain that I would avoid membership of the One Hundred Days Club.

The total membership of the One Hundred Days Club at the time of writing is forty-two crews, and is defined as any rower who has spent more than a hundred consecutive days on any ocean. I had been delighted when Tiny had delivered his prognosis that I was unlikely to join the twelve solo rowers and seven pairs who had taken more than a hundred days to row the Atlantic from east to west. It is arguable that these rowers are even more worthy of respect than their counterparts in the Sixty Days Club—those who have crossed the Atlantic in under sixty days—for what the

Hundreders lack in speed they make up for in perseverance. Being at sea for such an extended period of time brings its own hardships such as increased risk of scurvy, saltwater sores, and psychological difficulties.

But I was determined that I didn't want to be a member of this club, no matter how exclusive the membership. On the one hand I was trying to be philosophical, taking the attitude that I would get into Antigua when I was meant to get there and not a moment before. But Mr. Competitive, on the other hand, was still nagging me to push on so that I didn't slip into triple digits. It may have been foolish pride, but I desperately didn't want to be forever on record as a Hundreder. I knew it was entirely a function of how I chose to perceive the situation, but I couldn't help myself. I regarded Hundredship as a stigma to be avoided.

I had just finished what I called the sorry-for-myself shift, the first one of the day. My muscles were at their most sore in the mornings, stiffening up while I slept, but I would prize my protesting body off the bunk and start rowing while it was still dark, resolving not to start clock-watching at least until the sun had come up. I counted the strokes, gazing toward the east for the first glow of dawn, using the sunrise to distract myself from the stiffness of my fingers, the ache in my shoulders and lower back, and the pain of the saltwater sores that still plagued my backside. I had made progress psychologically. Now I could at least recognize that this was my regular time to feel sorry for myself, and was able to distance myself from the emotion of suffering by greeting it as a regular visitor—"Oh look, here's Mr. Self-Pity on his morning visit. How are you today, sir?"

On this day the first shift ended a couple of hours after sunrise and I returned to my cabin to write up my logbook. I turned on the chartplotter. Excitement! I was getting close enough to Antigua that now I could notch up the zoom on the chart to the next level of magnification and still see my boat and the island on the same screen.

But wait a moment. What was going on here? The line that led from my current position to Antigua stopped short of the island. The line was supposed to mark my course from here to the finish line, but it ended more than fifty miles to the east of Cape Shirley lighthouse. This couldn't be right.

With a sinking feeling in my stomach, I reached for the bound folder of race instructions, which I'd kept safely in a waterproof bag tucked behind my box of food rations. I needed to confirm the latitude and longitude of the finish. I had a horrible feeling that I already knew the answer. I pulled out the printed sheet with the yellow Woodvale header and found the information I was looking for: the finish line lay at 17 degrees north, 61 degrees and 43 minutes west.

I looked back at my chartplotter and pressed a button to view the latitude and longitude I had plotted for my final waypoint. 17 degrees north, *60* degrees and 43 minutes west.

Oh no. How had that happened? I had misplotted the position by one whole degree of longitude, which in this case was equivalent to fifty-eight nautical miles.* A few moments ago I had thought I had less than two hundred miles to go, but the depressing truth was that it was nearer to two hundred and fifty.

I was close to tears. So near and yet so far. This would probably add at least two days onto my estimated time of arrival, making it unlikely that I would get there before my hundred-day deadline.

---

* The imaginary lines representing degrees of longitude are 60 nautical miles apart at the equator, but converge as they go north and south until they meet at the poles. So the distance between the lines varies according to how far north or south you are. At 17 degrees north I was fairly close to the equator, so the distance between the lines was 58 nautical miles, or 69 statute miles (1 nautical mile = 1.15 statute miles).

Now I would have to average thirty-two miles a day rather than twenty-five. It was possible, but I would need the weather to help me, or I would have to cut down on my sleep and increase my hours of rowing. I had tried before to row more hours in the day, but it had just made me cranky and miserable with exhaustion. I wondered if I could manage it now that the end was almost in sight. What was more important—my sleep, or my pride?

At that particular moment, sleep seemed more important. I had survived the sorry-for-myself shift, and I now felt even more sorry for myself. I wanted my well-earned nap. When oceanic life became too much, sleep offered a way to make it all go away for at least a while. Drink and drugs do the same, but those weren't available to me right now. I curled up on my bunk for a twenty-minute escape into dreamland. I would figure out my strategy afterward.

The problem, of course, was still there when I woke up.

I resolved to row more hours, although it was the last thing my aching body wanted. I would try it for three days and see what mileage I could make. Then I would reassess the situation.

My resolution lasted less than twenty-four hours—until midnight that night. I had rowed for sixteen hours and covered a meager twenty-six miles. The night was overcast and pitch dark. I was aching, tired, and forlorn. I stowed my oars and skulked into my cabin, pausing only to write up my position in my logbook with the comment, "Sorry, can't do it, won't do it. Too dark, unproductive, sore arse. Sod it."

My mood wasn't much better when I got up at four the next morning to begin rowing again. I recorded my feelings in my logbook: "Boil on bum worse. Food running low. Will this nightmare never end?"

twenty

SO NEAR AND YET SO FAR

*E*ver since I had completed the final round of repairs to my oars, around the halfway mark of the crossing, I had been praying that the wind would rise and give me a helpful push toward the end of the race. I had heard reports that other crews had found wind, waves, and current lining up and propelling them at three to four knots toward the finish line, and when my phone was still working correspondents had assured me that I, too, would one day find this happy alignment of the elements that would send me surfing toward Antigua. Oh, how I yearned for that happy day! But it seemed that the earlier crews had used up the ocean's full ration of generosity toward ocean rowers, and as Day 100 approached, I found myself slogging along through a labyrinth of capricious currents, making barely one and a half knots.

Progress was depressingly slow, but Antigua was now just over a hundred miles away, and I was starting to believe that I would actually make it. Throughout my voyage I had entertained fantasies of my arrival, but so as not to tempt fate had always mentally added the caveat "*if* I make it." Now I was daring to think "*when* I make it."

But the Atlantic had one final surprise in store for me.

On my 101st day at sea, the wind turned against me—or so I thought. It felt as if it was coming from the east, but there was definitely something pushing me south. Antigua lay a few miles to the north of my present latitude, so south was the last thing I wanted. Anxious not to lose any of my hard-won miles, I decided to put out the sea anchor to see if it made any difference. It did— but not the kind of difference I wanted. My rate of southerly movement increased. Not good. I must have run into an adverse current, and now, thanks to the sea anchor, that current now had a nice big twelve-foot parachute to grab hold of, rather than just a small smooth hull. I had inadvertently harnessed a wayward ebb that was pulling me in the wrong direction.

As soon as I realized what was happening I went to pull in the sea anchor, but it wouldn't budge. It was like having a tug-of-war with an elephant. After hauling in frustration for several minutes to no avail, I concluded that the tripline had somehow got tangled around the main line, or around the parachute itself, so no matter how hard I pulled on the second line the sea anchor would remain inflated with its full payload of seawater. In effect, it was as if I had a ball and chain attached to my boat. I was stuck.

I couldn't think of any way out of the situation but to keep trying, so for about twenty minutes I tried hauling on the line, only to lose any progress I was making when the next big wave would come along and jerk the line out of my hands. This clearly wasn't working. I was going to have to try applying some intelligence to the situation—if brawn wasn't working, I would try brain. I hit on the idea of pulling on the tripline and after every few feet tying a quick slipknot in the rope. I could then clip this loop into a carabiner clip attached to a D-ring on my boat, preserving what I'd achieved. I made quite good progress in this manner, especially if I coordinated my hauling with the timing of the waves so that I pulled when the line went slack between the crests—heave (wave), heave (wave), heave, tie a knot and clip—and before long I had the sea anchor almost at the side of the boat. But there my progress stalled. When I had started pulling, the anchor was far away and the angle of the rope to the boat was shallow so I wasn't fighting gravity. Now that the anchor was just a few feet away, I was trying to pull in an upward direction and gravity was getting the better of me. I had lost weight during the voyage, the sea anchor had literally a ton of seawater in it, and in this unequal battle I simply was not strong enough to lift it.

I was considering this impasse when I caught sight of a passing ship, the first one I had seen since the *Pomeroy* just over a week before. I had been on the lookout for several days, hoping to get a message to Woodvale to make sure they knew I was getting close to land. I wanted them to be on standby in the likely event that I would need a tow for the last few miles into English Harbor if, like many of the other crews, I found that the wind had carried me too far north or too far south. Now I also wanted to get word to them about the problem with my sea anchor. I guessed the lack of progress and the unexpected southerly set of my course would be causing some puzzlement and even anxiety on dry land. So when I saw the other vessel I dove into the cabin to hail them on the VHF radio.

While I was explaining who I was and what I needed done, I looked out and saw that the tripline, instead of being clipped into the carabiner, had snapped. Just a frayed end of rope dangled from the D-ring. The situation was going from bad to worse, and a weary resignation overtook me. I finished my conversation on the radio, asking the other crew to pass on my message to Woodvale, and went out to have a look. The sea anchor was back out at the full stretch of its hundred-yard rope. I had lost all the progress I had made, and was now in an even worse situation because the tripline was gone and the main rope to the sea anchor was too thick for me to clip it into the carabiner.

What to do? I considered my options.

I didn't want to swim out to the sea anchor to investigate. As the *Sun Latte* crew had found to their cost, there were sharks out there.

I tried hauling in the sea anchor using brute force. Without being able to clip it into the carabiner there was no possibility to take a rest when I got exhausted. After fifteen minutes of struggling, I had achieved nothing apart from a great deal of damage to my hands, since the rope's friction stripped the skin from my fingers every time a large wave struck.

I could maybe row up to the sea anchor to relieve the pressure on the line. I tried. But after half an hour of battling into the waves and failing to make a single yard of progress, I conceded defeat.

I could cut the line to the sea anchor, consigning it to a watery grave, but quite apart from the environmental considerations, I would then have no means of preventing myself from being blown backward if I encountered an adverse wind between here and Antigua. There was also the problem that I had now lost the trip-line and also the third, emergency line that led from the main rope back into the cockpit. This meant that in order to cut the anchor free I would have to gain access to the point where the main rope connected with the boat—and it was attached to the towing eye right on the prow of the boat, at the far end of the smooth, curved roof of the forward cabin. I hadn't enjoyed crawling across this roof in the dead calm of La Gomera's marina when the roof was dry and still. Now it was wet and slippery, and being pitched around by twenty-foot waves. The notion of losing my grip and slipping off into the water, with sharks lurking, filled me with dread.

I was so tantalizingly close to land, and yet so far. Until I figured out how to escape from this predicament, I was being pulled farther and farther south, ever more distant from Antigua. My thoughts started to spiral into panic. I couldn't believe this was happening—yet another obstacle between me and my destination. Surely I had suffered enough out here. I had been on the ocean plenty long enough; nearly two months had passed since the winners of the race had crossed the finish line. I thought I had developed a philosophical acceptance about my plight, but now that I was faced with yet another delay I realized I had really, truly had enough. All I wanted was to feel my feet on dry land. But the ocean seemed to have other ideas. I railed against the unfairness of it all.

"Who promised you fair?" chided Mr. Competitive. "Quit your whining and deal with it."

I snapped to attention. He was right. I had to find a way to cope with this panic that was threatening to cripple me. I sat down on my rowing seat, facing the bow—toward the rebellious sea anchor—and took several deep breaths. Let's try and get this in perspective, I told myself.

You think this is tough. What have you done before that you thought was tough? Was it as bad as you feared? And are you still here to tell the tale?

As soon as I asked myself these questions, I knew the answers. And I knew that I could cope with this crisis, because I had coped before and I would cope again. I had come so far in the last three months. I would not be thwarted now. In my mind's eye I looked back at the me that had started this race—a timid, apprehensive me who lay quaking in her bunk fearing that the boat would disintegrate in the force of the waves; a doubtful me uncertain of her ability to cope with breakages and come up with practical solutions; a me with low self-esteem who constantly questioned whether she was capable of looking after herself in this alien environment. Without a doubt, at the outset this challenge had been too big for me, but I had grown into it, slowly gaining the confidence that I could succeed. I had achieved so much already, was I really going to let a stupid sea anchor stand in my way?

I stood up again, and looked at the roof of the forward cabin. It no longer looked so daunting. And maybe there was a way I could reduce the risks. I could rig up a safety line. There was a cleat on the topside of the cabin, just this side of the pointed prow. If I could make a loop in a rope and lasso the cleat . . .

I had never been much good at fairground hoopla, so I congratulated myself when after a mere twenty attempts I managed to get the bowline around the T-shaped cleat. I secured the other end of the line to a grab handle in the cockpit, and voilà! I had a safety line set up across the roof of the cabin. I could put on my safety harness and clip myself onto the safety line with a carabiner.

But I was still reluctant to cut off my sea anchor. Besides not wanting to leave debris in the ocean, it was worth about £500 ($1,000) and I could ill afford to lose it.

It was getting late in the day. I decided to sleep on it. If I hadn't come up with a better idea by morning, I would venture out over the cabin roof and cut the line. I retired to my sleeping quarters and tried not to dream about sharks and drowning.

The next morning dawned grim and gray, and the seas were rougher still. When I checked my position on the chartplotter I saw that, frustratingly, I had been pulled even farther south overnight. It was time to be free of my ball and chain. I pulled the yellow-handled diver's knife from its sheath, mounted on the bulkhead just inside the exit hatch of my cabin, and braced myself for action. Like it or not, I was going out over the cabin roof.

I stood at the fore end of the cockpit and contemplated the challenge. *Sedna* pitched and yawed ceaselessly in the rough seas. The rolling roof of the forward cabin was only about six feet from end to end, but six feet had never looked so far.

But I was going to do it, and I figured I might as well make sure that the moment was recorded for posterity. I had put clothes on specially for the occasion—a white T-shirt and navy Lycra shorts. I took out my video camera, slotted its monopod into a vertical metal tube on the roof of the aft cabin placed there especially for the purpose, and pressed the record button.

I rummaged around in a deck hatch and took out my safety harness, made of wide black webbing straps, and put it on over my T-shirt. I took a carabiner and clipped it to the front of the harness, then clipped it again onto the safety line that I had rigged across the cabin roof. I put the diver's knife between my teeth, like a pirate about to board an enemy ship, and left the safety of the cockpit. As I crawled out over the roof it bucked and swayed like a bronco.

I was no farther than halfway along the roof when I felt myself slipping sideways. I couldn't yet reach the cleat, and the safety line was not taut enough to stop me sliding off. My torso jackknifed sideways as I slid feet-first into the water, the safety line pulling sideways with my bodyweight. I felt a moment of panic, but trusted that my safety line would hold. As it brought me up short, a wave tipped the boat toward her bow and the carabiner slid along the safety line toward where I wanted to be, at the prow. The black line to the sea anchor was now within reach. It was not ideal that I was half in, half out of the waves, but I could manage. I realized I was breathing hard and took a few slow, steadying breaths to calm myself. Staying where I was, my body suspended in its harness from the safety line and my feet dangling in the water, I took the knife from between my teeth and sawed at the thick rope as *Sedna* lurched from side to side and up and down. The knife was sharp, and with a few strokes of the blade I had severed the line. The frayed end dropped into the water, and my sea anchor was lost to the deep. If I could, I would have held on to it and dragged it with me back on board, but I faced a big enough challenge just trying to get myself back to the cockpit. I put my foot on the yellow grab line that looped through rings fixed to the sides of the boat, and placing most of my weight on it I reached up for the safety line and pulled myself up out of the water. Stepping sideways along the grab line I made my way along the side of the cabin and swung my leading foot around into the cockpit. I reached for a convenient handle and pulled myself to safety.

I had done it. I was free of the sea anchor, free to row the last few dozen miles into Antigua. I punched the air in triumph and let out a whoop of victory.

For in cutting the line to the sea anchor I had liberated myself from far more than a yellow fabric parachute. I had fought my demons, and won. It was time for an exorcism. I acted it out in my imagination.

"Where are you, you scurvy scoundrels?" I roared. "Come here and walk the gangplank!" I lined them up along the starboard gunwale—Mr. Self-Doubt, Mr. Guilt, Mr. Self-Critical, and Mr. Competitive, the four sneering spirits that for so long had made my life so miserable.

"You, Mr. Self-Doubt, did you see what I just did? I had a scary situation, but I formulated a plan, took steps to mitigate the risk, and accomplished my goal. I succeeded. I *can* deal with a crisis. I can think it through and act sensibly and rationally. I *can* look after myself!

"And you, Mr. Guilt, there's no place for you here. I've got nothing to feel guilty about. I'm succeeding in my objectives, I'm doing my best, and that's all that anybody can ever do."

I turned my ire on Mr. Self-Critical: "You thought I was inadequate, that everyone would think me a fool, that I wasn't up to the challenge I had set myself. You thought I'd overreached myself, you didn't believe I could make it to the end. But you were wrong. I'm so nearly there, and nothing is going to stop me now!"

And lastly, to Mr. Competitive. "You were more insidious. Sometimes I thought you were on my side, spurring me on, but now I can see you didn't really help me at all. You were conspiring with these other guys to rob me of peace of mind. In reality, I was competing with nobody but myself, and my standards are the only standards that matter. The race is irrelevant—I have achieved what I set out to do, which was to conquer myself. And to conquer you! Be gone, the lot of you!"

And with that I kicked them one by one into the water, ignoring their feeble protests and self-justifications. They had plagued me for too long, and I wanted them out of my life. I took up my oars and rowed away as fast as I could, without a backward glance, leaving my demons to perish along with my sea anchor in the rolling waters of the Atlantic.

twenty-one

THE HOME STRAIT

$\mathcal{N}$ow nothing stood between me and Antigua but forty miles of ocean. I could almost smell the land. I was keeping a tight rein on my excitement—I still had to keep rowing every last yard—but completion now seemed achievable. The ocean had presented many surprises over the last three and a half months, but surely now the end was in sight.

It seemed unlikely that I would make it into English Harbor unassisted, as I was still sixteen nautical miles south of it and the wind was coming from the northeast, trying to push me yet farther south. I was making some northerly progress by angling as much as I could across the waves, but it looked as if I would run out of Atlantic before I managed to get far enough north. This was a relatively minor concern. After 103 days at sea, my main priority was to get off this uncomfortable little prison of a boat and back onto dry land, and if a tow was necessary, then so be it. Better that than to miss Antigua altogether.

I had no idea what kind of welcome might await me. Ever since the race had started I had used fantasies of a glorious arrival to motivate myself, but I had no idea what would happen in real life. I had been careful to remind myself after every happy daydream that the reality would probably be much more mundane. So I counterbalanced my more extravagant imaginings with visualizations of a humbler welcoming committee—maybe nobody other than my mother standing on the dockside, waiting to see me in. We would hug, exchange a few words, then I would go off for a hot shower and we'd get a bite to eat. Either outcome was fine with me. Just get me off this boat!

It was now the morning after the severing of the sea anchor. I had put in a solid twelve hours at the oars the day before. I had considered rowing all night to try to make enough progress north to reach English Harbor, but since I had become a fully signed-up member of the Hundred Days Club I had adopted a very laissez-faire attitude to objectives and timetable. I would get there when I got there, all in good time.

Still, it would be nice to get there today, preferably in daylight hours, and ideally before the end of the working day in Britain so that those who had been loyally following my sedate progress from their office computers would know for sure the moment that I arrived safe and sound in Antigua.

THE LAST DAY: 0400

And so here I am, wide awake and rowing. The sun isn't up yet, but the air is mild. I am wearing a baseball cap, and a two-piece of matching crop top and Lycra shorts for when the *Aurora* comes out to meet me. I feel the sense of occasion that comes when an era is drawing to a close. The last breakfast, the last sunrise, the last day.

0500

I take a slug of coffee. I haven't drunk much coffee on this voyage but now I feel the need for speed. I have no hot water since my stove broke, and the coffee granules have welded themselves into a solid mass due to the dampness of the ocean air, so I just pour a small amount of cold water into the canister, swill it around for a moment, and when it has dissolved enough coffee to turn brown I chug it down.

Euurgh! The cold, concentrated liquid makes me shudder. But it gives me the kick I need. I wash it down with a caramel syrup chaser to give me a quick sugar fix. I am in a hurry and I don't want to waste time eating and drinking, so this will do. I return to the oars.

0600

As I squat over the bedpan I notice that I have become thinner. Hollows have appeared where I have never seen hollows before— on the inside of my elbows, at the sides of my knees, in my armpits. The day before yesterday I shaved my armpits for the first time in several weeks, wanting to be presentable for my arrival in Antigua. I noticed that it was hard to get the wide, flat razor into the deep hollow under my arms. I notice that the skin on my stomach now wrinkles loosely, leanly. The fat is gone. I'm intrigued by these strange but welcome changes in my body.

I row on. "I'm tougher than most, tougher than most." "With every stroke, a little bit closer, a little bit nearer to Antigua." So close now. Surely.

0700

I can see Antigua! I stop at the top of the hour to update my logbook, and when I stand up from the rowing seat I see a hazy silhouette, surprisingly steep on either side, crouching on the horizon. The end is literally in sight. *Aurora* appears alongside to escort me in.

0800

Fast running out of Atlantic. Can I make enough north to get into English Harbor unassisted?

0900

Another slug of coffee. Do I really need it? I am so high on barely suppressed excitement now. It is a perfect day—sunny and bright. The only thing that could be better would be if the wind would turn from due east to a southeasterly, to blow me north toward English Harbor. I have the VHF radio on, and overhear *Aurora* giving an ETA of 1800. That's too late—I want to be there before that. I cancel all rest breaks until further notice.

1000

Antigua is getting bigger as I draw ever nearer. I am rowing powerfully. Despite all the caffeine and sugar I feel serene and calm. And strong. Nothing can stop me now.

1100

I am being swept southwest too fast—between one and a half and two knots. I'm not going to make English Harbor.

1200

I have a VHF conversation with Lin Barker on *Aurora* to arrange a tow. Without a tow I would skim by the south coast of Antigua, missing my landfall. Lin is going to call the harbormaster. I am still rowing well. My skin is salty. I had got used to my mint and tea tree sponge baths after each three-hour rowing shift, but today there is no time to spare for even my superefficient five-minute bathing routine. I am going to get to land without a moment's delay.

1351

I cross the line that signals the end of the Atlantic Rowing Race. When I am getting close, the *Aurora* goes ahead of me and waits at the precise line of longitude of the Cape Shirley Lighthouse—the official finish point. I count down what I think are the last one hundred strokes. But I'm not there yet, still not level with *Aurora*. Will this ocean never end? I count another hundred. Then another fifty-six, and at long last *Aurora* sounds her Klaxon. It is over. I have done it. I stop rowing, and stand up, and cheer, and holler, and bellow for joy.

I HAVE DONE IT!

A rigid inflatable boat (RIB) comes bouncing over the waves toward us. This is my ride into English Harbor. Mum is on board but I can't reach her for that long-awaited hug. "We did it, Mum!" I shout. She smiles at me. She is beaming proudly. I know that my words have expressed what she already knew—that I could not have done this without her help—and she appreciates the acknowledgment. The harbormaster throws me a rope and I tie it to my bowline. I remind myself to tie it well—I don't want any embarrassing mistakes at this stage. The harbormaster offers me a ride on the RIB, warning me that it may be uncomfortable on *Sedna* while she is being towed, but I choose to stay on board. She and I have come this far together—and together we will see it through to the end. Mum and I exchange greetings, but words cannot convey how we feel right now. Once the towline goes taut, she is too far away to speak to. I am now being drawn back to land, back to so-called reality. I stand on my boat, looking out over the bows toward Antigua, exulting in the glow of accomplishment.

We are going so fast. My hat blows off into the foaming wake—my loyal baseball cap, which along with my wide-brimmed sunhat and my fleecy nightcap made up my headgear wardrobe. My much-loved hat, which I lost overboard once before until the waves brought it back to my outstretched hand, now gone forever. But now I am Zen—unattached to objectives, unattached to material things. I go into my cabin to find another baseball cap. I put it on.

Now we are drawing close to the island. Boats come out to greet us—yachts, motor cruisers, more RIBs. I can see the silhouettes of people standing along the clifftops. Over the noise of the waves, and the din of the wind rushing past my ears, I can hear the sound of boat horns, people cheering.

As we reach the harbor, the harbormaster slows the RIB to a stop. "Would you like to row in by yourself?" he asks.

Yes, I would. This is how I had always pictured it—rowing into English Harbor under my own power. He unties the line and once again it is just me, *Sedna*, and my oars. I am grinning from ear to ear as I approach the dock. The din is deafening. Air horns are blaring, people are cheering, and I can hear children singing, a timid melody almost drowned out by the cacophony. After months of nothing but the sounds of wind and water, the sound of humanity is music to my ears.

As I near the quayside I stop rowing and turn to face the crowds, letting my boat drift the last few feet. I am amazed at the size of the throng. White and brown faces, children and adults, all smiling, all cheering. They are all here for me! I am so happy. I love them all. I have been almost totally deprived of human contact for so long, and now I feel a huge wave of love for my fellow man. These are my favorite people in the whole world! They have come to see me in, and I adore them for it.

A fizz of champagne hits me in the face. Somebody has uncorked a bottle and is spraying it over me in a traditional victory salute. It gets in my eyes and makes them sting, but I don't care. I care more that I haven't had a drop of alcohol in 103 days and now the precious liquid is being wasted on my skin instead of down my throat. Not to worry—I step ashore and instantly someone presses a beer into my hand.

But hold on, I haven't even had a sip of the beer yet and I already feel drunk. The ground is lurching uncontrollably beneath my feet. What is happening?

After so long on an erratically tipping boat, my body has grown accustomed to the movement, and now that my feet find themselves on firm ground the adaptation is working against me. Friendly hands reach out to steady me as I wobble.

And there is something else amiss. Where is Mum? From the midst of the crowd I look around frantically.

"Here she is," a voice reassures me.

And indeed, there she is. The crowd parts for her as she makes her way toward me. Somebody has handed her a burning marine flare and she carries the incandescent stick aloft, like the Statue of Liberty, as she approaches me, smiling.

So long we have waited for this hug. So many times she sent me this hug down the telephone line, as I bobbed around in my tiny boat and she reached out to me from her humble home in England. So many occasions when she felt so powerless to help, and all she could offer me was the promise of a mother's embrace. So much we have both grown in strength and self-belief, since we last hugged in La Gomera, an ocean and an eternity ago.

We hug.

twenty-two

AN ALTERED REALITY

*a*fter so many days of seeing nothing but sea and sky and a little silver rowboat, the colors and smells of Antigua seemed ultra-vivid, and the onslaught on my senses was intense.

For the first hour or so after I landed there was a succession of speeches and presentations from various local dignitaries, wanting to shake my still very sore hand and present me with mementos of Antigua. A choir of schoolchildren sang a song specially adapted for the occasion: "From my window late at night / I can see the rowboat's flickering light." I stood uncertainly on my feet, bracing my legs and wishing the ground would stop swaying. I was slightly bemused by everything that was going on, but it didn't matter. I couldn't stop smiling. I had made it. At last I was in the promised land.

When the presentations were over the crowds melted away and Mum and I were left standing on the quayside, wondering what to do next. I was still bubbling with excitement and emotion (and caffeine), but after so many months of rowing, I didn't know what to do now that there was no more rowing to be done.

Somebody had tied my boat alongside the quay, and I was

assured that she could stay there for now while I went to my hotel. This would be the first time in months that I had parted company with *Sedna,* and it felt strange, as if I was suffering an amputation. Already beginning to feel nostalgic about our time together, I gave her a sentimental pat on the cabin roof and turned my back on her.

My legs didn't seem to be cooperating with my brain, so Mum helped me to the Admiral's Inn, a beautiful old building just a few yards away. I knew that once, a long time ago, I'd been pretty proficient at this walking thing, but I seemed to have forgotten how.

I tottered up the dark wooden staircase to my room, and felt as if I had stepped into heaven. It was exactly as I had pictured it during those long hours of daydreaming on the ocean—an elegant, airy space, with a four-poster bed that was almost as big as my boat. A gentle breeze blew in through the slatted window shutters and fluttered the white muslin curtains. My ocean life seemed a million miles away, apart from this one thing—I still had the driving rhythm of my rowing mantras running through my head. "Tougher than most, tougher than most." "It's OK, brain, you can stop now," I pleaded. "I'm on dry land. I can stop rowing. Stop it. Please!" But the rhythm continued relentlessly, and would do so for a couple more days before my nervous system registered the fact that my row was finally over.

I peeled off my salty sports bikini and inspected myself in the full-length mirror on the bathroom door. This was the first time in months that I had seen myself in a mirror, and there was definitely a lot less of me than there had been the last time I looked. This was a good thing. I was very slim, but not painfully thin. And I was brown as a berry—or at least, most of me was. When I rowed I had always worn a hat, rowing gloves, and running shoes, so my forehead, hands, and feet were totally white, as was my backside and the backs of my legs. Because I had been in a seated rowing position whenever I was out of doors, I also had two white stripes across the middle of my tummy, where the skinfolds had been. The harbormaster later commented that all the rowers had arrived with these distinctive stripes—a quirky kind of badge of honor.

I stepped into the bathroom to take a shower. Ah, white fluffy towels! The epitome of luxury. When I had imagined myself arriving in Antigua my fantasy had extended as far as picturing the hotel bathroom—the first shower, the sweet-smelling toiletries, and big, white, downy towels. My dream was coming true, but the reality was even better. Everything was clean and nice, and soft and pleasant, and dry and comfortable—the opposite of everything that my time on the boat had been.

I turned on the shower and luxuriated in the jets of hot water. I washed away the salt, the stress, the struggles, and emerged from the bathroom feeling like a new woman.

Mum had brought the bag of clothes from England that I had prepared before I left. It had been hard to know what to pack. I had optimistically banked on losing weight during the crossing, and had packed my "skinny clothes"—the cute little garments that I had bought during my New York gym-junkie days while I was exercising myself into thinness. I hadn't been able to wear them for quite some time, since my pre-race bulking-up phase, and it would be nice to fit into them again. I zipped myself into a pair of navy Capri pants that even in my skinny days had been a snug fit. They slid straight down over my buttocks and landed in a heap around my ankles. I turned around and examined my rear view in the mirror. My bottom seemed to have disappeared. There was nothing there to hold my pants up. I found a skirt that fit and made myself presentable. I looked in the mirror and admired the effect. I looked slim, fit, and feminine. After so many months of being a rower, at last I was a woman again.

That evening I went out for dinner with my mother. We walked along the harborfront, me weaving slightly from side to side as the ground still rolled uncontrollably, until we found a restaurant with tables and chairs on an outside deck. It seemed strange to sit on a proper chair, at a proper table, with linen napkins, silverware, and wine glasses. I was grateful that the chair was cushioned, a welcome relief for my bony and boil-ridden backside. I perused the menu, enjoying the novelty of having options after such a long time on a diet restricted to what I had on board. Ah perfect. My choice was clear. "Seared tuna steak, with salad and ginger dressing, please. And a glass of chilled Sauvignon Blanc."

As we waited for the food I listened to the breeze rustling through the fronds of the palm trees overhead, and the chatter of the other diners. I stroked the linen napkin. All these sights and sounds, once so familiar and yet almost forgotten during the months I had been away.

The glass of wine arrived. I lifted it reverently to my lips. The first sip of alcohol I had had in three and a half months. Would I have lost my taste for it? No, evidently not. The dry white liquid tingled across my tastebuds. Delicious. When the food came I had to ask my mother to observe a moment's silence so I could appreciate the full sensory sensation without distractions. The tuna was perfect—rare and succulent. If food had ever tasted this good before, I had not fully appreciated it at the time.

When I was on the boat I had resolved that I would never again become blasé about the things that I had previously taken for granted on dry land—flush toilets, running water, hot food, shops and stores—but I also knew that it would be a miracle if I did not. It would be mentally exhausting to be constantly grateful for all the minutiae of life. But for now it was as if I were discovering all these things for the first time, and I would make the most of this happy phase of simple pleasures.

While we were eating, Mum outlined the plan for the week. She'd had to take a guess as to what date I would arrive, and when I should fly home. She had booked me a flight just seven days hence. I had been invited to the Island Academy to meet the schoolchildren who had been singing to me at the quayside today. We would have to get the boat cleaned up, cleared out, and made ready to be shipped. Various journalists wanted to speak to me. A local sailing/drinking society called the Tot Club had invited me to receive an award.

I felt the world crowding in on me. For so long my world had been my little rowboat. All I needed I had within arm's reach. All I had to do was row. All I thought about was the next shift, the next stroke. By contrast, life on land seemed complicated—a logistical challenge of deadlines and schedules and obligations. For the briefest of moments I yearned to be back out on the wide open ocean, where life was simple.

We had finished dinner by ten o'clock, and I went back to my hotel room. I should have been exhausted after a 4 A.M. start, ten hours of solid rowing, and enough excitement to last me a lifetime, but I was full of restless energy. I went to bed but was up again an hour later, pacing around on the matting of my room, wanting to go out and celebrate. I had missed my birthday, Christmas, and New Year's Eve while I was on the ocean, so I had a backlog of celebrating to catch up on. But there was nobody to celebrate with. I briefly considered going out on my own, but I gave up on the idea, returned to my four-poster, and slept until dawn.

The rest of the week passed in a kaleidoscope of happy memories. Antigua treated me like a celebrity, and I relished my brief period of comparative fame. There were free dinners from local restaurants, assembly at the Island Academy school, interviews with journalists from Britain and the Caribbean. A local spa gave me a complimentary full-body massage and a therapeutic session with a physiotherapist to help sort out the aches and pains in my back and shoulders. The crew of the 247-foot superyacht *Mirabella V* gave me a guided tour of their craft, and we did a photo shoot of my very little boat alongside their very large boat, over ten times the length of *Sedna* and a world away from her in terms of luxury—with sumptuous guest suites, onboard swimming pool, laundry room, and a professional galley with walk-in refrigerators. They both floated on water, but there the similarities between the two vessels ended. And everywhere we went, people would greet Mum and me by name, and congratulate me on my achievement. I was touched by the kindness and generosity of everybody we met. I had barely stopped grinning since I reached dry land—and my mother tells me I barely stopped talking, either.

But it wasn't all fun. I had to get *Sedna* ready to go into storage, and although boat cleaning was the last thing I felt like doing, it had to be done. Fortunately, a small team of Brits assembled to assist, and many hands made light work. With their help we found a boatyard willing to accommodate *Sedna* until she could be shipped to the United States, and we cleaned *Sedna* from stem to stern, scrubbing out hatches and laying everything out to dry in the hot tropical sun.

The harbormaster towed her across the bay to a lifting hoist so we could get her onto a trailer. Slings were put around her hull and she was slowly lifted from the water. I sat on the dockside, gazing in wonderment at this trusty craft that had carried me safely across three thousand miles of ocean. She looked so small, so fragile, so very vulnerable. It seemed incredible to me that we had made it. We had survived. I was not especially sentimental about *Sedna*— she was just a boat, a thing, and I certainly did not believe that she had a soul or a personality—but she had served me well. We had been through a lot together, although the relationship had not always been easy. I had cursed her, as I had cursed the wind and the waves and everything else on the ocean. She had been both life support capsule and prison cell. But the relationships forged in adversity have an intensity that fair weather friendships cannot match. *Sedna* had looked after me and got me safely to Antigua, and for that I was eternally grateful.

I felt the tears welling up—tears of intense emotion, a mixture of relief, wonderment, gratitude, and pride that I had survived and in what I had achieved.

After a week in Antigua I returned to London by airplane. As I sat in my window seat I looked down at the vast blue expanse of ocean thirty thousand feet below me and marveled at the scale of it. It had taken me three and a half months to cross it from east to west. Now it was taking less than nine hours to make the journey from west to east. Some people might regard it as perverse to choose a human-powered ocean crossing when technology had provided the means for a much cheaper, easier, and faster way of travel. But I had my reasons. I have rarely heard anybody describe a flight as a life-changing or character-building experience.

Soon after my return there was a fund-raising event held in my honor at the Royal Navy's shore establishment in London, HMS *President*. We raised over £10,000 ($20,000) for the Prince's Trust, my chosen charity. My ex-husband came along, as did a number of his friends, who had also become friends of mine. As I was making my short speech I looked over at this tall, handsome man who had been such a major part of my life. He was listening attentively, his expression one of mixed pride and puzzlement. He looked as if he were mystified by the transformation in this woman who had once been his wife, who though still recognizable now had a different aura about her—an aura of self-respect and increased gravitas. I realized that I still loved him, but that my priorities had changed since he and I had first met fifteen years previously. I had now found a new purpose in life, and although I had not been able to bring him with me on my journey I still wished him happiness. I had dreamed of him often while I was on the ocean, and no matter whether we were together or apart, I knew that he would always be a part of me.

Two weeks later I was once again on an airplane, this time bound for New York. I was due to give the after-dinner speech at a North American alumni event for my old Oxford college. I had been planning this speech, on and off, across half an ocean, and I was quite clear about what I wanted to say. As well as describing my adventures, I wanted to impart some of what I had learned on the ocean. I didn't want to preach—far be it from me to tell anyone else how they should live their lives—but I did simply want to describe the lessons that I had learned that had helped me get through the day, in the hope that they would resonate with at least a few members of the audience and might help them get through their own life challenges. I narrowed it down to three simple messages: when in doubt, just do it; be clear about your objectives and measure yourself only against those objectives, not somebody else's; and when the going gets tough, mentally travel through time and get the "retrospective perspective"—what seems so hard now will all be worth it in the end, or at the very least will make a great story to tell in the pub.

When I had worked in the City of London I had loathed public speaking. Even saying a few words in front of a handful of senior executives would make me tremble in fear and flush with embarrassment. I always dreaded that somebody would ask me a difficult question and my lack of knowledge would be revealed. But now I found I was looking forward to my speech. At last I had something to say, and I could be confident that I knew my material better than anybody else in the room. Yet even so, as I stood up to speak in that dark, wood-paneled room at the Harvard Club, I worried about how my motivational pep talk would be received. After all, most of the people attending the dinner were considerably older, wiser, and more accomplished than I. But I must have made some sense, because the commendations afterward were glowing, and I basked in the warmth of their praise. In adventuring and speaking I had at last found something at which I could be successful—I had found my life purpose, and it felt good.

EPILOGUE

*f*or much of that first week in Antigua I had felt as if I were dreaming and feared that I would wake up to find that I was still on my boat with another hard day's rowing ahead of me. Then I started to fear the opposite—that dry land would become my whole reality, and my time on the ocean would recede into the distance like a fast-fading memory. The race had been the hardest thing I had ever done, way beyond what I thought my limits were. I had experienced self-doubt and depression, solitude and soul-searching, sleep deprivation and pain. But despite all that suffering, or in fact because of it, it had been a precious experience and I didn't want to lose all I had gained.

The crossing had been far from perfect—I had made mistakes, had not lived up to my high expectations of how many hours I was going to row or how cheerful I was going to be. Of the twenty crews that finished the crossing from the original twenty-six, I had finished last, contrary to my hopes and wishes—but in the long run, none of these shortcomings mattered. What mattered was what I had learned along the way, and I knew that I had ended the voyage a happier, healthier, wiser person than I was when I had started it. And that, ultimately, had been my goal.

Toward the end of my voyage I had discovered a version of myself that I liked—a stronger, more capable, more self-sufficient version of the self that had pushed off from the Canaries. I admired and respected that oceangoing version of me, and I didn't want to lose touch with her. I wanted to bring back the best of her into the land-based me, to provide an inner kernel of serenity and strength that I could draw from in times of need. I had gone out on the ocean to find out who I was, but if that discovery could not survive the transition back to dry land, then the whole exercise would have been a waste of time.

But life can be hard. And can continue to be hard, even after you've rowed an ocean. The marine environment had been so different, so far removed from all the norms of dry land, that it had been relatively easy to let go of bad old habits and make room for new good ones. On the boat, it was not an option to be careless, or clumsy, or stupid, because the possible consequences would be so much more serious than on dry land. Back on dry land I was surrounded by all the same old situations, the same old stimuli, and it was all too easy to slip back into the corresponding same old life scripts. Temptation was on every side.

Just as I had once imagined, in my materialistic way, that life would be better when I lived in a bigger house, or remodeled the kitchen, or drove a newer car, for a while I fell into the equally fallacious belief that life would be better when I had rowed an ocean. My life is better, but only because I have worked at learning as much as I can from my experience. The Atlantic crossing, long though it was, encompassed such a wide range of trials—physical, mental, and spiritual—that the learning curve was too steep for me to fully comprehend the lessons while they were happening. It was like a crash course in personal development in which I never had enough time to do all my homework. As with many kinds of education, it was only after I had passed the "exam"—by arriving safely in Antigua—that I was able to reflect on my experiences and begin to make sense of them. And it was longer still before I was able to fully absorb those lessons into my daily life. It has been through an ongoing process of crystallization, speaking about those 103 days of solitude both in public and in private, and in writing this book, that I have come to understand the significance of my Atlantic adventure.

Despite what I have achieved, I don't for a moment think I am any braver or better than anybody else. This is how I attempt to explain what gives me the strength to do what I do; when that thunderbolt of an idea first hit me and inspired me to row across oceans, it filled me with a sense of purpose so strong that it overcame my fears. Even when boredom, frustration, fatigue, or despair threatened to overwhelm me, it was that powerful sense of purpose that kept me going.

But I am still very human, and I struggle with life the same as anybody else. I still find myself fighting pointlessly against things that cannot be changed. I still run into difficulties in relationships, get angry and frustrated, beat myself up excessively over my shortcomings, and face disappointments and setbacks. But that's how it goes. And the good news is that although I still occasionally spiral into despair, I am getting better at recognizing the symptoms, so gradually I am reducing the amount of time that elapses between getting caught in the whirlpool of negativity and breaking free from the vortex.

I have learned to be kinder to myself, to imagine that I am my own best friend, whispering comforting words in my ear and drowning out the voices of Self-Doubt and Self-Criticism.

I have learned to accept that, in the present moment at least, things are exactly as they are meant to be, and although I cannot control the future any more than I can control the wind and the weather, I can manage it and influence it in a positive way.

I have learned not to take things personally. Just as I eventually realized that the ocean was not being deliberately spiteful in order to punish me—it was just doing what oceans do, according to the laws of physics—so just the same, if people criticize me or judge me, it is not really about me; it is about them. They are acting according to the laws of their own personal physics, created by a life history of conditioned hopes, fears, and emotional triggers, which have nothing to do with me.

I have learned a lot, although sometimes I feel I have acquired just enough wisdom to know how much more there is to be learned. If my ego is ever in danger of running out of control, I only have to remember the feelings of complete helplessness I experienced at times on the ocean, and that cuts me back down to size. Compared with the awesome might and eternal power of the ocean, no human being can fail to be aware of their own insignificance.

I am still rowing oceans. As I write this I am one-third of the way through a solo trans-Pacific row, having recently become the first woman to row from California to Hawaii, and I plan to continue all the way to Australia after a suitable break to allow body, boat, and bank balance a chance to recover.

If I ever stop challenging myself, then I am getting lazy and comfortable and I am no longer growing. I hope to use life's challenges as stepping stones to ever greater things. I doubt if my challenges will always be quite so extreme but I intend to keep working toward an obituary of which I can be justifiably proud—to aspire, achieve, and advance, always striving to be better tomorrow than I am today.

This is my chosen path, and although it may not be an easy one, I cannot now live in another way. Since that moment several years ago, when I sat at the dining table contemplating the alternative futures written on two sheets of paper in front of me, I knew that my life was going to change. The thrill of excitement that I felt while I imagined my perfect future told me that I was onto something, and this was the direction I should be heading. Then, through trial and error and process of elimination, eventually I stumbled across a path that would take me there. No doubt there are other paths that I could have taken, and in the future I may come to a fork and choose to explore a different route—but the ultimate goal remains the same: to live the authentic life that I was born to live, realizing my true potential. Since I started down this track it has become a brave new experiment as I pursue my sense of curiosity and adventure. Every day brings surprises, some welcome, occasionally not so welcome, but each one a valuable learning experience.

When I look back to that sad and desperate woman who shut away the two contrasting versions of her obituary in a desk drawer, too timid to contemplate where it might lead, I can't help but wonder at how far I've come. It has been a long and winding route, but with remarkably few moments of real terror. A couple of times there was no option but to take a huge and sudden leap into the unknown—leaving my husband, setting out across the Atlantic—but mostly this transformation has happened, much like my Atlantic crossing, through the accumulation of many tiny actions, barely significant in themselves but adding up to a total turnaround in almost every aspect of my life.

I try to remind myself of this power of accumulation whenever I am faced with a daunting new challenge. I focus on the first small step I need to take in order to move one fraction of an inch closer to my goal. It might be making a phone call—or even just finding out the number, if making the call seems too intimidating for today. It might be making a list of actions—or buying the notebook in which to write the list. It might be reviewing the draft of chapter 1—or at least opening the document file.

Starting is always the hardest part, when the whole task lies ahead of me and the distance between me and my objective seems as wide as the Atlantic Ocean. But now I know that once I get started, momentum will gradually build.

Who knows, in the ultimate reckoning, if my life will be deemed a "success." Success or failure—that does not matter to me. What does matter is that I live every day knowing where I am going, and that my daily actions are taking me closer to that goal. To live a fulfilling life is an endurance event, and the only way to get to the finish line is to focus on the present, checking from moment to moment that I am still heading in the right direction. The Atlantic taught me that no matter how huge and seemingly impossible the task, anybody can achieve extraordinary things, by simply taking it one stroke at a time.

I recently heard a wonderful metaphor for the spiritual quest. It goes like this: when you stand at the bottom of the mountain and look up at the mountaintop, the path looks hard and stony, and the top is obscured by clouds. But when you reach the top and you look down, you realize that there are a thousand paths that could have brought you to that place.

For we are all on a great adventure—the adventure of life—and even for the majority who will never row across an ocean or climb a great peak or trek to a pole, there is much to be learned from living life with mindfulness and awareness. I chose ocean rowing because it was the best fit with the values and priorities I held at that point in my life. But parenthood, business, study, friendships, public service, meditation, and life in general can also teach us about what is important and what is not. My goal is to be happy, healthy, and wise—and ultimately isn't that what we all want?

ACKNOWLEDGMENTS

my heartfelt thanks to all the following, who have contributed advice, opinions, moral support, and, when required, alcohol—and to the hundreds of others who have helped me along my way, and to the thousands more who via the Internet have shared in my erratic journeys across oceans and through life in general.

Taryn Fagerness at the Sandra Dijkstra Literary Agency, who has been a staunch advocate of this book throughout its gestation.

My editor at Simon & Schuster, Kerri Kolen, for her support and reassurances when I was worrying over my book like a new mother over her infant.

Ellen Hawkes, who helped form the early drafts of my manuscript into something marketable. Thank you for all the sage advice and Sauvignon Blanc.

Karen Luscombe, Karen Morss, and Helena Smalman-Smith, for reading drafts and giving me greater confidence as I found my voice as a writer.

My wonderful boatbuilders: Richard Uttley, Tim Gilmore, and Sam Poore.

Other friends, supporters, and advisers: Bede Brosnahan, Briony Nicholls, Tiny Little, Dave Steer and Jane Hollis, Shaun

Bolster, Julian and Celina Hamm, Natalie Gotts, Leven Brown, Adrian Flanagan, Ricardo Diniz, Mick Dawson, George Simpson.

Also to all my sponsors: the Royal Navy, Green People, Mornflake Oats, Wholebake, Biocare, Waterrower, the Tiller School, Clipper Teas, Simrad, GComm, Besso, Ilium, Bushcraft Expeditions, Commercial Freeze Dry, Aquapac, ParadiseBet, Ondeck Sailing, 7E Communications, Rule Financial, Number One Health, Fourth Element, Fitness Exchange, Best Foot Forward, Webexpeditions, Kakadu Sports Gloves, Gazing Performance, and Colin Habgood.

Thanks also to the Royal Navy and The Prince's Trust, and my marvelous events committee: Rodney Byram, Alexandra Foley, Commander Mike Pearey, Sam Allpass, and Pauline Appleby.

All the friends, both new and old, who emailed while I was at sea, letting me know that out of sight was not out of mind, with a special mention for my ex-husband, Richard, whose influence has helped form the happy person I am today.

And of course my long-suffering mother, Rita Savage, whom I appreciate more with every passing day for her never-ending love, support, patience, and ability to refrain from telling me I'm a complete idiot.